LEGEND

MEMORIAL   AUDITORIUM

The American Legion

AIR MAIL
TOMORROW'S MAIL TODAY
EASTERN AIR LINES

1st trip via
CHATTANOOGA
Inaugurating
new Line
Friday, May 1st 1936

Ernest
George Fa
Eddie Ste
H. P. Litt

A B Cea
427 E
Chatta

...essee's Postmaster
...bra asst Postmaster
...S. Mgr., Lovell Airport.

21235

UNITED STATES POSTAGE
U.S.A. AIR MAIL
6
6
CENTS
TENN.

...rke

...5th St

...ooga

Tenn

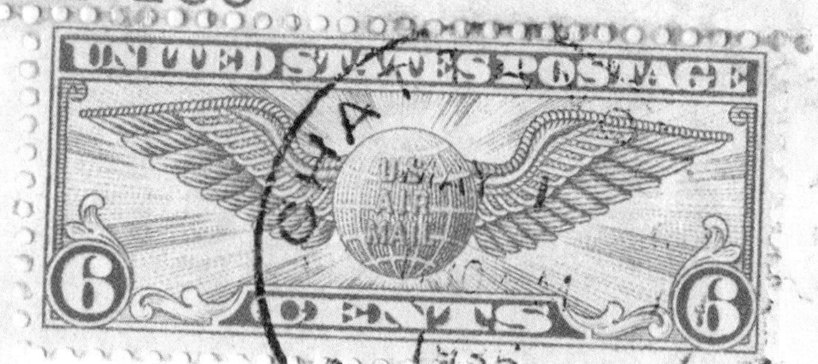

LEGEND

PHILIP KAPLAN

To the designers, engineers, administrators and especially,
to the ordinary workers of Douglas Aircraft, who built the fabulous DC-3.

First published in Great Britain in 2009 by
Peter Livanos and Philip Kaplan

Distributed by Vine House International Ltd
Waldenbury,
Chailey, East Sussex BN8 4DR

British Library Cataloguing in Publication Data.
A catalog record for this book is available from
the British Library.

ISBN 978-0-9557061-1-0

The majority of proceeds from the sale of *Legend*
are donated to SOPARA — Support Our Paras.

Preceding page: C-47A N1944A, before the recent re-painting.

Printed and bound in Singapore.

AMERICAN AIRLINES
AMERICAN AIRLINES
FLAGSHIP
NEW YORK
GOLDDIGGERS 1937

TEXT AND DESIGN	PHILIP KAPLAN
PRODUCTION	GEOFF BARLOW
COPY EDITING	MARGARET MAYHEW
EDITORIAL CONSULTATION	TONY BIANCHI
	TOM WOODHOUSE
SPECIAL THANKS TO	PETER LIVANOS
	ANDREW DAVENPORT
	JOHN DODD
	QUENTIN BLAND
	NEAL KAPLAN
	RACHEL CONNOLLY
	FRANCO TAMBASCIA
	C LACHMUND STURM
	PAUL VAN DEN BERG
	ERIK SLEUTELBERG
	DOUG SIEGFRIED
	ERIC HOLLOWAY
	HAN GEURTS
	OZ FREIRE
	JAMES MCMASTER
	FERGUS MAYHEW
	ANN AND JOHN TUSA
	NIKLAS AHMAN
	JOHN HEGGBLOM
	GEOFF LEA
	JERROLD WU
	JUHA KLEMETTINEN
	LARS DANIELSSON
	HENRY HOLDEN
	MICHAEL KOMINIK
	SIGIDUR BENEDIKTSSON
	STEPHEN FOX
	SIMON THOMAS
	DAMIEN BURKE

CONTENTS

MORNING SUNLIGHT ON
CAPTAIN AKE JANSSON'S
DC-3, 9Q-CUK, AT
HAMBURG IN 2007.

FOREWORD

Like the Spitfire, and a relatively small number of other classic aircraft, the DC-3 / C-47 / Dakota is a breed apart, distinguished not only by her exceptional design, engineering, durability, performance, and her many other fine characteristics, but by her enormous base of admirers. To the millions of people who have been her passengers and the enthusiastic captains and crews who have operated her for more than seventy years, to her countless fans in the aviation world and those whose lives have been affected by her in the most dramatic ways, she is unforgettable.

Without question, the great Douglas plane changed history, opening the era of modern air travel in the 1930s and as the backbone of Allied air transport in the war. In its Santa Monica, Long Beach and Oklahoma City plants, Douglas Aircraft produced 10,349 of the planes. More than 2,400 additional examples were built by Japan and Russia, both under licence and without such permission.

Her lineage began with the DC-1, a low-wing all-metal (except for the fabric-covered control surfaces) monoplane that first flew in July 1933. The DC-1 offered enclosed passenger accommodation, trailing-edge flaps and retractable landing gear. She was the prototype for the DC-2 production model that led to the Douglas Sleeper Transport, whose first flight came in December 1935. The DST had sleeping berths for sixteen passengers and, though only built in a small run, made a great impression on transcontinental night flights. It evolved into the DC-3, whose maiden flight from Clover Field, Santa Monica, California, on December 17th 1935, marked the beginning of a major revolution in air travel. This came on the 32nd anniversary of the Wright Brothers' pioneering flight at Kittyhawk, North Carolina.

With the entry of the United States into the Second World War, the U.S. military realized that, in the DC-3, it had a truly important multi-purpose transport aircraft that would be crucial to the Allied war effort. Oddly, it would also become the only plane to be operated by every major combatant on both sides in that war. Built and flown by both the Soviets and the Japanese, the American DC-3—now designated C-47—was flown by the Germans as well. They formed a fleet of such aircraft captured from various airlines during the Nazi blitzkrieg campaign.

A significant surviving veteran of the war, the C-47A N1944A, is an impressive example of the type. Her wartime squadron code was J8-B and this historic plane was completed at the Douglas Aircraft Company, Long Beach, California plant on February 14th 1944. With only two hours and fifty-five minutes flying time on her airframe, she was accepted by the U.S. Army Air Force on March 1st. By late May she was based in England at AAF Station Upottery in Devon, one of the key D-Day launch bases of the 101st Airborne Division "Screaming Eagles." Upottery was the base of Lieutenant Richard Winters and the men of Easy Company, 506th Parachute Infantry Regiment, the subjects of the book and television series *Band of Brothers*. From Upottery, J8-B was among eighty-one C-47s to participate in the airborne assault on Normandy of June 6th, bringing their paratroopers to the landing zones of northern France behind Utah beach.

In 2008 the European Union ended the passenger-carrying career of the greatest, most significant Allied workhorse of the Second World War, the marvellous, ubiquitous Douglas DC-3 (the Dakota to most Britons.) This magnificent twin-engine airliner went to war all over the world in the 1940s as the C-47, playing a vital role in that conflict, helping to win it and to liberate millions of Europeans in the spring of 1945. General Dwight Eisenhower, in his book *Crusade in Europe*, wrote: "Most senior officers regard as the most vital to our success in Africa and Europe the bulldozer, the jeep, the two-and-a-half-ton truck, and the C-47." None of them had been designed for their combat role.

In its 175-page EC Regulation 1899/2006, the EU declared a new set of requirements for all passenger-carrying aircraft that operate in European Union countries. The directive fails to distinguish between modern airliners and the rather small, vintage aircraft like the DC-3, which are seen mainly at airshows and similar events. It demands that all passenger-carrying airliners must now be fitted with escape chutes (to deliver DC-3 passengers to the ground four feet below the exit door), passenger oxygen masks (for aircraft that never fly at altitudes where supplemental oxygen is needed), and other equipment normally found in a jumbo jet. Such additions are both prohibitively expensive and fundamentally impractical for the old, reliable DC-3, several hundred of which are fully airworthy around the world, many of them still earning their keep on a daily basis. Does this legislation really mark the end of passenger flying in this fine old machine? Is it really the death knell for her in the job she was created to do seven decades ago? Rules can be changed, if and when sufficient and appropriate reason is applied.

In *Legend* the fascinating wartime and post-war history of the C-47, N1944A, is traced, along with the pre-war, wartime and post-war story of the DC-3 / C-47 type.   - Philip Kaplan

DOUGLAS

In 1959, Donald Wills Douglas, Sr. wrote that, for most of the preceding forty years, his time and energy had been devoted to the design and manufacture of commercial and military aircraft. He also observed that in 1921 none of the Douglas Aircraft family watching the take-off of the Douglas "Cloudster" on its maiden flight could have predicted the scores of marvellous designs that would roll from their assembly lines in the years to come. "A few of our designs attained some degree of fame, and one of them, the DC-3, has become almost legendary. It seems to go on forever. More than ten thousand of these transports were built, several thousand remaining in service today, and representing a twenty-five year span of service. It is fairly safe to predict that a few of these hardy veterans will be flying twenty-five years from today." It was. Today, nearly fifty years after his prediction, many DC-3s continue to earn their keep in private hands, hauling passengers and cargo, as flying reminders of the impact the DC-3 has had on the world since that first flight on December 17th, 1935, the thirty-second anniversary of the Wright brothers' controlled powered flight at Kittyhawk in North Carolina.

Born in Brooklyn, New York, on April 6th, 1892, Douglas was, from an early age, excited by the achievements of the Wright brothers and other aviation pioneers. When, in 1904 at the age of twelve, he read an account in *Aeronautical Journal*, of the Wrights' flight, it set him on course to become one of those pioneers himself.

The summers of his childhood were spent at his family's home on Long Island Sound where he learned to sail. Sailing became a life-long passion for Douglas and he would probably have made a career in the U.S. Navy were it not for his father taking him to the National Museum at the Smithsonian Institution in Washington DC, where he was fascinated by an exhibit on the Langley Experimental Aircraft Engine. From then on it was flying machines that held his interest. Douglas was witness to many of the Wright brothers' experimental flying exercises at Curtiss Field on Long Island. Many years later he told friends that it was this link to the Wrights that firmly fixed him on course to his aviation career. Ironically, a book on flying machine construction appeared in the United States during 1910 containing the quote: "In the opinion of competent experts, it is idle to look for a commercial future for the flying machine."

Donald Douglas emerged from prep school in 1909 and, in deference to his father, entered the United States Naval Academy at Annapolis in Maryland. He had little spare time as a lowly midshipman, but what he had he spent watching the further experimentation of the Wright brothers with their aeroplanes, then at Fort Meyer, Virginia.

After trying unsuccessfully to persuade the school officials to institute a course in aeronautical studies, he resigned from the Naval Academy and enrolled at the Massachusetts Institute of Technology, which had just established such a curriculum. There he earned a Bachelor of Science degree in only two years. After graduating he worked for a year with Jerome Hunsaker, his mentor at M.I.T. and the man who had developed the aeronautics course there. With Hunsaker, Douglas created an early wind tunnel device for evaluating aircraft design performance. He went on to his first job in the fledgling aircraft industry, working on the DN-1, the first dirigible for the U.S. Navy, with the Connecticut Aircraft Company at Trumbull Airport, Groton-New London. From there he met and went to work for Glenn L. Martin for whom he designed the Model S "hydro-airplane." But the First World War was about to begin and Douglas soon felt compelled to leave Martin to accept an appointment in Washington as chief civilian aeronautical engineer for the U.S. Army Signal Corps. Douglas: "I think I can truly lay claim to being one of the very first of the aircraft engineers. Until that time, there was no formal engineering. It was all done by judgment. If the airplane flew, the judgment was good. If it didn't, the judgment was bad." In less than a year, however, Douglas had become so frustrated by Army red tape and procedural delay that he resigned and returned to the Martin Company who were delighted to have him back.

With the Martin design team Douglas began to flourish as his work on the revolutionary MB-1 Martin Bomber quickly confirmed the superiority of his design over that of any American or European competitor. In the war years Douglas created the Martin MB-2 as the standard Navy and Marine bomber of the next ten years, leading to the beginning of strategic air power

for the United States. In the MB-2 Donald Douglas envisioned something beyond its military application: an airframe that, without any important structural changes, could easily carry twelve passengers or a ton of mail. Douglas: "Speed is the most outstanding present-day advantage of the airplane. I rank passenger-carrying first in importance. Correspondence, or the telephone cannot supply the complete satisfaction of actual personal contact. Where any great distance separates the subject and his objective, present-day express train service often proves too slow. Commercial operators must take the risk. One way or another they must carry passengers on schedule, comfortably, and without a mishap for a reasonable period. Where speed is of the very quintessence of transportation, the airplane will have a definite field and a profitable one."

But in the early 1920s, the United States lagged behind Britain which, by 1920, had already flown more than 4,000 passengers and almost 60,000 pounds of cargo nearly 85,000 miles with efficiency and without injury or loss of goods.

One legacy of the post-World War One years was the expanded knowledge and capability in the field of aircraft design and manufacture. The demanding requirements of weaponry had

dramatically accelerated the evolving industry and greatly advanced the state of aircraft technology. The American economy, however, fell into decline as, almost overnight, more than $100 million in government orders for aircraft were cancelled after the armistice ending "The Great War." The U.S. aviation industry ground to a halt amid stockpiles of 10,000 brand new military aircraft and many thousands of Liberty aero engines. In less than six months, twenty-one of the twenty-four most important aircraft-related companies in America were out of business, affecting some 200,000 of the industry's skilled workers. The unused aircraft were on the auction block at bargain prices.

Within the economic chaos of the industry, the Glenn L. Martin Company survived, largely due to the clear superiority of the Douglas-designed bomber. Its quality had made the reputation of the company, helping it to prosper even in that toughest of times. And in the gloom Donald Douglas saw the most significant opportunity of his lifetime. Confident in his capability and design ideas, he left Martin for the second time, and took his young family and meagre savings to sunny Santa Monica, California, and the western end of Wilshire Boulevard, the Pacific Ocean edge of the Los Angeles sprawl. There he would

establish Douglas Aircraft which, by the height of the Second World War, would be the fourth largest company in America. In the 1920s it was a desk in a tiny space at the rear of a southern California barber shop.

The only other aircraft maker on the west coast was William Boeing in Seattle. Boeing's business had dried up entirely after the war and he was reduced to manufacturing bedroom furniture. Such were the prospects that awaited Douglas on his arrival in the west to pursue his "opportunity." He faced a major hurdle in his efforts to secure financing and investment in an era of little public interest in the prospects for commercial aviation. Sceptics in the financial community were quick to point out that aviation was immature and had not as yet demonstrated a capacity for safe, responsible, organized operation.

While struggling to find financial support for his new company, Douglas happened to meet a wealthy, adventurous young man named David R. Davis. The two got on well. Davis, who wanted to try for the unattained non-stop cross-country flying achievement, commissioned Douglas to build a new plane for his attempt. With the enormous sum of $40,000 in his pocket, Douglas quickly hired five of his former colleagues at Martin to

FAR RIGHT: CHIEF ENGINEER ARTHUR RAYMOND, DOUGLAS AIRCRAFT, WHO ADVANCED THE DEVELOPMENT OF THE DC-3 AND MANY OTHER DESIGNS OF THE COMPANY.

RIGHT: PROFILE VIEWS OF THE THREE PIONEERING ALL-METAL DOUGLAS TRANSPORT DESIGNS OF THE 1930S.

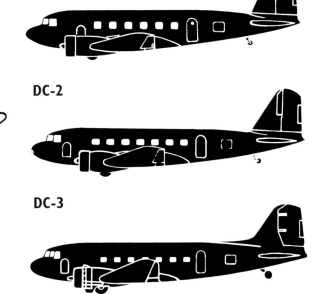

DC-1

DC-2

DC-3

join him in California on the Davis project. They were all non-plussed when they arrived outside the little barber shop, but most of them would remain with Douglas for the rest of their careers.

The aircraft they designed and built was the Cloudster—a large, two-place wood and fabric bi-plane, thirty-five feet long with a 56-foot wingspan, powered by a 425 hp Liberty engine. It had a range of 2,800 miles and was one of the few aircraft in aviation history capable of lifting a combination of payload and fuel equal to its own empty weight. Former Martin chief test pilot Eric Springer flew the Cloudster for Douglas. With clear sky and a relatively good weather forecast, Springer and Davis took off from Goodyear Field, east Los Angeles, in the early morning of June 21st 1921, bound for Curtiss Field on Long Island, New York.

A mechanical failure forced the pair to land at Fort Bliss, Texas, where the craft was then severely damaged in a passing thunderstorm. After structural repairs, the Cloudster was flown back to California for complete engine repair, and during this delay the trans-continental non-stop record was claimed by a U.S. Army Fokker T-2. The revamped Cloudster would, without the further involvement of Douglas, become his first commercial aircraft. Refitted with ten seats and expensive trim, the plane was operated briefly by T. Claude Ryan, whose San Diego-based aircraft company would later design and build the Spirit of St Louis

for Charles Lindbergh. In 1926, the Cloudster came to an ignominious end while hauling a load of beer to Tijuana, Mexico. An emergency landing was successfully carried out but the pilot failed to secure the plane properly for the night and by the next morning the high tide had battered it to destruction. David Davis went on to become famed as an aeronautical expert and designer of the revolutionary "Davis Wing," used in the Second World War by Consolidated Aircraft on their B-24 Liberator bomber and some of their flying boats. The new wing gave the Liberator 20 percent additional lift and enabled it to carry an additional 8,000 pounds of payload.

On August 2nd 1932, Donald Douglas opened a letter from his old friend Jack Frye, Operations Vice President for Transcontinental and Western Air Inc (TWA), who asked if Douglas would be interested in building ten or more tri-motored transport planes for TWA. The little Douglas Aircraft company had been keeping busy in the development of some important aeroplane projects. One of them was an aircraft specially designed to make it possible for the United States to be the first nation to complete a flight around the world. This aviation achievement seemed to arouse great public interest.

In 1919 a U.S. Navy NC-4 aircraft had successfully crossed the Atlantic, and in 1922 British airmen John Alcock and Arthur

Whitten-Brown had tried without success to circumnavigate the globe in a Vickers Vimy. In the next year a French attempt failed and a second British effort was organized and then abandoned. In July 1923, U.S. Army officials began planning a route for a globe-circling flight to be attempted the following year. Major General Mason M. Patrick was in charge of the operation.

The goal was: "To show the feasibility of aerial communication and transportation between the various continents; to make the people of the world conscious that aerial transportation is able to meet any and all conditions under which it might be forced to operate; and to arouse interest in aircraft as a vital force in the markets of commerce." The plan called for U.S. Army Air Service personnel to set the specifications and conduct the actual flight and the army came to Douglas for the aircraft it would need. The Air Service ordered four of the planes and a prototype fifth aircraft, and over the course of their design and construction it heavily hyped the flight and the contribution of Douglas Aircraft, raising the awareness, interest and enthusiasm of the public.

In order to achieve the goals, the planes had to be designed as either land or water-type craft and would be called the Douglas World Cruisers, the *Seattle*, the *Chicago*, the *Boston*, and the *New Orleans*. They had no radios or advanced navigational aids, only the standard instrumentation of the time.

The Air Service had chosen four of its best pilots for the

flight: Major Frederick L. Martin, Flight Commander, Lieutenant Lowell H. Smith, Lieutenant Leigh Wade, and Lieutenant Erik H. Nelson. Each pilot had selected a mechanic/co-pilot to accompany him on the flight. In the planning, refuelling and repair sites were established at key locations along the route and the cooperation of the U.S. Navy and the Royal Air Force was secured.

Following successful trials, the four aircraft were lined up at Santa Monica's Clover Field on March 17th 1924 as thousands of people gathered to watch the 7 a.m. take-off. Unfortunately, a thick fog had rolled in from the Pacific and it was 9:35 before conditions had improved enough for the flight to begin. The planes took off and headed north towards Seattle where the actual round-the-world attempt would start on April 5th. Fog would again prevail and the start had to be deferred until the next morning when the four aircraft departed at 8:47 on their historic journey.

Weather conditions proved treacherous for the flight as rain, snow, sleet and powerful headwinds kept the crews struggling to stay in the air and on course, but over a period of 175 days the flight managed to cover the 27,553-mile route, with an actual flying time of fifteen days, eleven hours and seven minutes. Two of the four World Cruisers were lost in the effort. The *Seattle* crashed into a mountainside in Alaska after the crew became disoriented in fog. The aircraft was destroyed but the

American Airlines INC.

Bitte

13 JUILLET 1924

MEETING D'AVIATION

14h ORGANISÉ PAR L'AÉRO-CLUB D'ALSACE AVEC LE CONCOURS DU 2me RÉGIMENT D'AVIATION DE CHASSE, DE M. PAULET, PARACHUTISTE, ET DES AS LES PLUS CONNUS. — CONCOURS PUBLIC DOTÉ DE PRIX EN ESPÈCE 14h

STRASBOURG

LA GUARDIA FIELD RESTAURANTS

NEW YORK MUNICIPAL AIRPORT

EXAMPLES OF THE POST CARD,
MATCHBOOK, AIRLINE TIMETABLE,
CIGARETTE CARD, POSTER AND
OTHER AVIATION ART OF THE 1920S
AND 1930S.

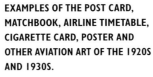

VUELE POR PLUNA
PRIMERAS LINEAS URUGUAYAS DE NAVEGACIÓN AÉREA

UNIENDO PUEBLOS HERMANOS!...

227:—OFF FOR A TRIP ON UNITED AIR LINES, LA GUARDIA AIR PORT, NEW YORK

47732

pilot and mechanic survived. The three remaining World Cruisers crossed the northern Pacific "relatively uneventfully" via Japan, China, Indo-China, Siam, Burma, India, Persia, Asia Minor, the Balkans, and France, where they were welcomed by massive crowds at Paris before proceeding to London. Trouble came early in their North Atlantic crossing, however, when the *Boston* lost oil pressure, was forced down at sea and damaged beyond repair while being lifted aboard a naval vessel. Again, the crew survived. With only two World Cruisers remaining in the flight, the prototype was summoned to join them at Pictou, Nova Scotia, where it was named the *Boston II*. The planes then continued on to Seattle where the record flight had begun.

When they finally landed triumphantly back at Clover Field in Santa Monica, more than 200,000 spectators were there to welcome them home. From that moment, the international reputation of Donald Douglas and his aircraft company was made. Today, the restored World Cruiser *Chicago* is displayed at the National Air and Space Museum, Washington DC, while the *New Orleans*, the other survivor of the record-breaking flight, is part of the collection of the Los Angeles County Museum of Natural History.

The accomplishment of the Americans in the round-the-world flight is still appreciated as one of the great feats in aviation history; however, it was not done without significant sacrifice. Two of the four principal aircraft were forced down and destroyed. The crews survived other forced landings, a range of terrifying weather conditions, mechanical difficulties requiring many repairs, indescribable fatigue and a variety of minor mishaps. But the achievement advanced the cause of eventual worldwide air transport.

The resulting publicity of the flight also advanced the cause of Douglas Aircraft, which almost immediately received a U.S. Army contract for fifty planes based on the World Cruiser design—an award worth $750,000, which was a huge sum at that time. With the business, of course, came major new expenditures, ranging from an increased payroll to larger space for manufacturing. The site chosen by Donald Douglas for his new location was that of an abandoned Santa Monica movie studio on Wilshire Boulevard, now a small urban green space known as the Douglas Park Municipal Bowling Green.

The visionary Donald Douglas moved on from his work for the army, focusing on what he believed to be the pathway to commercial air transport. He designed and built fifty-nine mailplanes for the post office. Of these primitive but well-engineered craft he later stated: "These early structures, designed expressly to carry the mail, were the foundations for the DCs that were to come." It seemed clear that he was heading in the right direction. Mail delivered by air took half the time taken by the railroads to cover the same distance. But there were problems. The lack of adequate navigational aids and instrumentation meant an inordinately high attrition rate for pilots flying the mail. In 1925, the U.S. Government put the delivery of air mail in the hands of private operators, but by then thirty-one of the original forty pilots who had started the air mail service in 1920 had been killed in crashes.

The federal Air Mail Act of February 1925 would lead to the advent of true commercial air transport service. By making it possible for the fledgling air carriers to offset most of their expenses through the carriage of mail, the Act opened the door a crack to the potential of air passenger travel. Douglas: "I built mailplanes because I couldn't sell people on the dream I had from the beginning. I knew the day was coming when everybody would want to travel by air but I had to wait."

The next major action along that pathway to commercial air transport was the passage of the Air Commerce Act in May 1926. This groundbreaking legislation provided regulations for the examination and licensing of pilots, aircraft, communications, enforcement and accident investigation. The age of flying purely by luck, skill and the seat of one's pants was coming to a close as improvements in instrumentation, communication, and safety devices introduced a new level of responsible operation that was intended both to protect and impress the travelling public. It brought with it the new Department of Air Commerce, a forerunner of the Federal Aviation Authority. Public trust and enthusiasm for flying was further enhanced a year later with the first solo flight across the Atlantic, when Charles Lindbergh, a young air mail pilot, flew the Ryan-built *Spirit of St Louis* from Roosevelt Field, New York, to Le Bourget, Paris. The popular Lindbergh became known as "Lucky Lindy" and "The Lone Eagle," inspiring Americans and others around the world to want to fly.

By the time Lindbergh flew the Atlantic, Donald Douglas had outgrown the Wilshire Boulevard building and was looking for

larger facilities in the area. Clover Field was only about a mile away and there was land for sale on the site. Douglas found the acreage he needed on the north boundary of the field, purchased it and began construction of a large new factory. Those were boom times with many people riding high on a wave of prosperity—a wave that was soon to break. By 1928, the young airline industry had confidently grown to more than forty companies offering scheduled flights in various parts of the U.S. The Air Commerce Act was two years old and air transportation was burgeoning. Unfortunately, so too were airliner crashes—twenty-four of them with fatalities. Fifty-three such aircraft had been destroyed in accidents of various kinds, and in 1929 alone, the year of the great stock market crash, there were fifty-one airliner crashes with sixty-one fatalities. The glamorous adventure of air travel had lost much of its glitter by the end of the decade. Even so, Douglas kept his work force busy in the turbulent recession years, and managed to turn a profit. His company's reputation for building exceptionally sound, well-constructed aircraft continued to grow. With his move to the new Clover Field facility, he was employing an engineering staff of more than 200. The company was grossing $2 million a year and, within the aviation industry, was second in value only to the much larger United Aircraft conglomerate.

With the passage of the McNary-Watres Act in April 1930, the U.S. Postmaster General was able to establish an integrated airline industry. The individual airlines were paid at a fixed rate for their cargo space to carry air mail and that rate would gradually diminish over the next five years to require the airlines to wean themselves from the subsidy and generate self-sustaining profit through the carriage of passengers. The Act further enabled the Postmaster General to combine or extend airline routes when doing so was deemed to better serve the public interest. Walter F. Brown was serving in that capacity at the time and shared with Donald Douglas the view that airlines in future should primarily be carrying passengers rather than putting their priority on mail. The problem was that no existing aircraft operated by the airlines was capable of carrying a full load of passengers as well as enough mail to be in profit within the existing rate schedule. This was the circumstance in which the first of the Douglas line of commercial airliners was conceived.

One further event served to accelerate the coming of the commercial air transport revolution. On March 31st 1931 a TWA Fokker tri-motor transport crashed in a Kansas wheat field after abruptly ending communication with a ground station. The two pilots and the six passengers, including Knute Rockne, the revered football coach of Notre Dame University, were killed. An investigation was opened but rumours quickly spread about the cause of the crash which had cost the life of the celebrated, high-profile Rockne. Public confidence in the young airlines of America was badly shaken. The aircraft design of the renowned Antony Fokker was suddenly controversial and, within a year, the major airlines had scrapped their Fokker aircraft.

TWA replaced their Fokker planes with nineteen Ford Tri-Motors beginning in November 1932, but was operating the Fords so extensively that the aircraft were rapidly wearing out and needing replacing after an average of 3,200 flying hours.

In Seattle, the Boeing Company was showing signs of recovery from its worst days in the 1920s, having designed and produced the XB-9 for the army, a well-received bomber. To enter what he saw as the promising market for civilian air transport, William Boeing had a B-9 bomber modified as a comfortable, modern airliner. The Boeing 247 was carpeted, heated, and well-insulated to greatly reduce the noise level in the passenger cabin from that of the Fords and Fokkers. The new twin-engined all-metal, stressed skin 247 was seen as a vast improvement for passengers and a powerful tool for recapturing the disenchanted air travelling public. The safer, better-instrumented airliner performed impressively—about 20 percent better than its Ford predecessor.

The first customer to buy the $68,000 247 was United Airlines, who shrewdly tied-up Boeing's production of the new plane by ordering sixty of them, thus eliminating direct competition from other major airlines wanting their own 247s. Boeing would not be able, for example, to provide 247s to United's competitor TWA for at least two years, until the United order was completed. Desperate for new and competitive airliners, TWA could not wait for such long-delayed delivery from Boeing, and it was then that Jack Frye, the TWA vice president for operations, wrote to Donald Douglas to ask if Douglas Aircraft would design and build a minimum of ten new tri-motor transports for his airline.

Jack Frye was a colourful character. He had come from Texas, been a cowboy, a flying instructor and a stunt pilot in the movie industry of the 1920s. He had started his own airline, Standard Air Lines, which catered to the stars and the wheeler-dealers of Hollywood. He had prospered and, when Western Airlines bought his airline, a new airline called TWA (Transcontinental and Western Air) emerged after the Standard acquisition. Frye was made a vice president of the new line and became the youngest airline executive in America.

It was during the desperate climate of economic depression in the early 1930s that Donald Douglas determined to make a place for his young company in the immature but promising commercial air transport market, then largely supported by the travels of business executives. Until that point, Douglas had been building observation planes for the army, but he was concerned that there was not enough military business for the various plane makers of the time. This further motivated him to crack the commercial market. Thus, the arrival of Jack Frye's letter on August 2nd 1932 provided the opportunity Douglas needed and he welcomed it. Frye wanted ten or more new all-metal monoplane tri-motor transport aircraft with a top speed of 185 mph and a range of 1,000 miles. The new plane had to carry twelve passengers and be capable of taking off, fully loaded, on two of its three engines. He asked for engines that were super-charged and capable of reaching a service ceiling of 21,000 feet and of maintaining 10,000 feet on any two of the engines. Frye was urgently seeking to outdo what his competition was offering its customers.

Douglas immediately turned to Arthur Raymond, then his assistant chief engineer, to help him meet the Frye request. Harvard graduate Raymond had also attended Massachusetts Institute of Technology where he had studied for a Masters Degree in Aeronautical Science before trying his hand unsuccessfully in sales during the 1920s. He had got a job with Douglas, filing tubular fuselage fittings, though his real calling was in engineering. Six weeks later Douglas had received the army contract for the 0-38 observation planes and needed additional engineers quickly. On learning that he already had a promising one—Raymond—right there in his own machine shop, he transferred the young man to his engineering staff on a salary of $30 a week. Within a decade, Arthur Raymond would become chief engineer, second only to Douglas himself in the chain of command, when James H. "Dutch" Kindelberger left that position to accept the presidency of General Aviation Manufacturing Corporation. Kindelberger would later head North American Aviation and preside over the development of the highly successful Texan/Harvard trainer, the B-25 Mitchell medium bomber and the P-51 Mustang fighter.

At first, Raymond was sceptical about the requirements Frye had laid out in his letter to Douglas. Douglas and Raymond then met with Kindelberger, Douglas's executive vice president, Harry Wetzel, the Douglas general manager, Fred Herman, project engineer, and assistants Lee Atwood, Ed Burton and Fred Stineman. The group agreed to pursue the challenge from TWA and to having their ideas for the new plane on paper within a week. Despite the three-engine requirement, the Douglas team was determined to find a solution that called for only two engines, which meant that for safe operation the plane would have to be able to maintain flight and altitude on a single engine.

One week later, armed with their written proposal for the new aircraft, Raymond and Wetzel left Los Angeles by train for New York City to meet with Frye and the TWA president, Richard Robbins. They chose to travel by train, partly because the lengthy journey would allow time for polishing their proposal figures, and partly because neither man was comfortable with the cost, relative danger, and unreliability of commercial air travel in 1932. When the pair sat down with Frye and Robbins they were joined by the renowned Charles Lindbergh who was then serving as technical advisor for TWA. Lindbergh showed immediate concern about the bi-motor aspect of the Douglas proposal. "If an engine should fail on take-off, we want to be able to climb out with a full load on the remaining engine. If you're going to build a bi-motor, as your drawings indicate, we still want the engine-out requirement. We want to be able to climb to an altitude of 8,000 feet, the highest point on our route system, and maintain level flight on the one engine. If you can do it, we'll buy the design. If not, we'll go elsewhere." With the very future of Douglas Aircraft resting on his response, Raymond said, "We can meet your requirements."

Arthur Raymond had championed the two-motor design

because by eliminating the nose engine, visibility for the pilot and co-pilot was improved and there was less noise and vibration and no fumes in the cockpit. He became convinced that through properly shaping the plane, using stressed-skin all-metal construction, and the right engines, Douglas could almost certainly do the job. But he was later quoted, "We had no idea what we were getting into when we began designing the DC-1."

Frye and Robbins prevailed upon Raymond to return to Los Angeles via Kansas City in order to work with TWA technicians on the detailed specifications for the new airliner. This time he did travel by air. He wanted to evaluate the Ford Tri-Motor aircraft that TWA was then operating. The trip proved an eye-opener for him. "I took off from Newark at 9 a.m. and bumped along all day at a low altitude, arriving over the Mississippi at dusk. It was amazing! I had seen the Atlantic and the Mississippi on the same day. It was raining and after dark when we landed at Kansas City. When we touched down I got a spray of muddy water on my feet from the S-shaped fresh air ventilators. I made a mental note not to use that system on our design. I knew then why people took the train."

After ten days of intense discussion with the TWA people in Kansas City, Raymond returned to Douglas Aircraft in Santa Monica with a bundle of the airline's specifications for the new plane. They included such requirements as: "Each surface control, ailerons, rudder, elevators and flaps shall be replaceable by two men in ten minutes," "It shall be possible to remove and replace complete landing gear and shock units by one man in one hour," and "The complete instrument panel shall be removable by one man in twenty-five minutes, exclusive of auto pilot."

Kindelberger placed Raymond in charge of the DC-1 project and his first important decision was the hiring of Bailey "Ozzy" Oswald, to handle the key performance calculations that would find a way to create the plane TWA was demanding. Oswald was told it was only a temporary assignment, but, in fact, he would remain with the company until his retirement.

Many at Douglas, including Donald Douglas himself, harboured occasional doubts about their decision to opt for a two-engine design for the new airliner. But when Douglas mentioned the concern to Kindelberger, Dutch dismissed it with, "Who would buy a plane that even looked like a Ford or Fokker?"

As the Douglas design team attacked the problem of the DC-1, they had the benefit of Arthur Raymond's comments and reac-

PRECEDING SPREAD: UNITED AIRLINES INTRODUCED THE FIRST AIR STEWARDESSES IN THE EARLY 1930S. HERE, NEAR THE ENTRANCE OF A BOEING 80A TRI-MOTOR AIRLINER ARE, FROM LEFT, MARGARET ARNOTT, INEZ KELLER, CORNELIA PETERMAN, HARRIET FRY, JESSIE CARTER, ELLIS CRAWFORD AND, IN THE DOORWAY FROM LEFT, ELLEN CHURCH AND ALVA JOHNSON. CHURCH WAS UNITED'S FIRST STEWARDESS. ALL NURSES, THE YOUNG LADIES FLEW THE CHICAGO-SAN FRANCISCO ROUTE OF BOEING AIR TRANSPORT, AN EARLY DIVISION OF UNITED.

LEFT: AN AMERICAN AIRLINES FLIGHT HOSTESS IN CHICAGO DURING 1938.

tions after his trip to Kansas City in the Ford Tri-Motor, which included his thoughts and recommendations about cabin temperature control, soundproofing, seating, lavatories, and other comforts.

Among the greatest influences in the development of the DC-1 was that of the brilliant and pioneering aircraft designer Jack Northrup, who had worked for Douglas until leaving to take a position with Lockheed in 1927. Northrup had developed a radical new multi-cellular wing design that, in one version or another, had been adapted by many aircraft manufacturers of the time. The wing offered exceptional strength and it received approval for use on the new Douglas airliner. With it came important reductions in both weight and internal cabin noise.

In the universe of aeroplane makers there was little experience of building all-metal aircraft in the 1930s. The craftsmen had to use extremely labour-intensive methods. After studying the engineering drawings, they drew their patterns on aluminium sheets and then hand-shaped the metal using blocks and mallets. Nearly everything about the DC-1 was new and had to be invented or designed from scratch, stretching the imaginations and creativity of the makers to new limits. The standard transports of the day, like the Ford and Fokker tri-motors, were high-wing designs with fixed landing gear. For efficient, maximum performance, the DC-1 would have retracting landing gear, though not fully retracting. For safety, it was decided that the main wheels would extend halfway out of the engine nacelles when retracted so that, in a wheels-up emergency landing, the partially exposed wheels would help to cushion the landing, as would the large, low-wing of the new plane. In later years, incidences of forced landings by DC-3 descendants of the DC-1 proved the wisdom of this landing gear innovation.

Forecasting the performance of the DC-1 decades before the advent of computers was limited to wind tunnel testing, mock-up fitting and static ground-testing of the airframe and completed aircraft. These primitive efforts to learn about the characteristics of the radically new design were remarkably accurate means of determining flaws, faults and unsatisfactory aspects of the design, months before it would enter actual flight testing. The research, of course, added considerably to the overall cost and investment of Douglas in the project, but the money was well spent in that it identified problems early that would otherwise have only been discovered in flight. The research and testing served to prove (and disprove) the mathematics applied in the design. One example was actual instability which was then corrected in the wind tunnel testing by means of a new wing sweepback, general reconfiguration and an adjustment in the centre of gravity. Another instance of wind tunnel-inspired design improvement came when it was found that a new design for the wing flaps resulted in thirty-five percent improved lift and 300 percent increased drag—radically improving the landing speed profile of the big plane. Yet another example of gain achieved through testing was the revelation that adding a fillet between the wing and fuselage brought an additional seventeen miles per hour to the top speed. A further twenty-seven mph was added through several more minor design adjustments. In another case where the testing produced a dramatic improvement, it was found that positioning the engine nacelles well ahead of the wing leading edge made it possible to locate the landing gear main wheels forward of the centre of gravity. This significantly improved the stability of the DC-1. So important and valuable were the results obtained through the wind tunnel, mock-up and static ground-testing work on this first of the DC airliners, that such testing became normal industry practice on all future aircraft of Douglas and of other principal aeroplane makers.

The Douglas engineers wanted a practical means of test-fitting and trying the many and varied components of the DC-1, so they built a full-sized mock-up, covering wood frames with heavy paper to represent the aluminium skin—the first such full-scale mock-up to be used in the commercial air transport industry. Raymond, "We designed the seats so they could flop over like those in an old trolley car. The seats were a tubular construction and not at all good looking or comfortable by the later standards of the DC-3. I picked out a horrible brown that would never have won any prize. We didn't know very much in those days. Early attempts at colour coordination looked like a psychedelic nightmare." After much experimentation, trying the positioning of the seats to find maximum comfort and roominess, it was decided to position each reclining seat opposite a window, forty inches from seatback to seatback, mounted on anti-vibration rubber pads. The seats had ample leg-room and were next to a relatively wide, unobstructed aisle. Unlike the other airliners of the era, a six-foot-tall passenger could walk fully upright through the cabin.

Another specific requirement of TWA was that the cockpit be designed in such a way that the pilots could reach out to clean the windows. Jack Frye and TWA chief test pilot Tommy Tomlinson personally took charge of the layout for the cockpit instrumentation, spending countless hours in the mock-up trying various permutations of instrument, switch, dial and handle positioning until they were satisfied that they had achieved the most practical and efficient arrangement. This accomplished, they had a lighted instrument panel installed and then devoted hours to the problem of predicting and eliminating or reducing unwanted reflections in the cockpit during night flying. It was only later, however, that they discovered the single most dangerous reflection produced in DC-1 night operation—that of the nose-mounted landing light which, in snow, haze and fog would produce a reflection that could be confusing or even blinding for the pilots.

Arthur Raymond, meanwhile, was concerning himself with passenger-related considerations such as noise, heat and ventilation. The unpleasant memories of his flight in the Ford motivated him to look for new and better ways to cope with these concerns. Raymond called in Sperry Corporation's Dr Stephen Zand, a specialist in aeronautical acoustics, to consult in the development of the DC-1. Zand knew that the engine clatter, vibration and propeller noise in the Fords and Fokkers produced a noise level of more than 100 decibels in the passenger cabin, making conversation or sleep difficult. He began experimenting with a variety of soundproofing matcrials including one called Seapak, which was composed of layers of Kapok under the duralumin skin of the aircraft, next to a layer of panelling made of a combination of rubber and balsa wood, all within a fabric covering.

CONTROL TOWER

LAND LIGHTHOUSES.

POSITION FINDING.

vent in the nose of the plane. The circulation of cabin air provided a complete change of air every sixty seconds, with a 70 degree cabin temperature maintained even when the outside temperature descended below zero.

With these innovative solutions applied, and the bulk of component and layout plans agreed, TWA gave final approval to the mock-up in mid-March 1933, enabling construction of the DC-1 to begin. It soon became obvious that with the various additions and innovations being built into the new plane came a substantial increase in its empty weight, which had been contractually agreed at 14,600 pounds. That number had risen to 17,000 pounds and some of the Douglas engineers now believed that the take-off weight had become unacceptable. This problem was partially resolved when the west coast representative of the Hamilton Standard Propeller Company convinced Arthur Raymond that the new controllable pitch propeller his firm was then developing would let a DC-1 pilot adjust the angle of the propeller blades efficiently for enhanced performance in all situations, including the take-off.

Power for the DC-1 was selected after a bizarre competition between aero engine makers Wright and Pratt & Whitney. The two powerplant companies were allowed to set up work areas opposite each other in the Douglas facility and each struggled to gain an advantage over the other in a race to win the engine contract. The offerings of both firms came with significant disadvantages: the Wright engine was hampered by a cylinder head cooling problem, while the entry of Pratt & Whitney burned oil excessively. The ploy of pitting the two engine builders against each other on site in the plant eventually produced the result that Donald Douglas was after. An exceptionally fine powerplant had been re-engineered and refined to meet the needs of the DC-1. The engine contract went to Wright and, ultimately, two-thirds of the 10,632 DC-3s built would be powered by the Wright Cyclone engine, while all military C-47 versions were powered by the highly successful 1,000 hp Pratt & Whitney Wasp engine introduced two years after the competition with Wright for the DC-1 contract.

Somewhat larger than its rival, the Boeing 247 airliner, the Douglas DC-1 first appeared outside the company assembly building on June 22nd 1933 and was greeted with excitement and anticipation. The beautifully streamlined fish-like airframe came with many improvements over the Boeing plane and met

He found that, at a speed of 185 mph, the noise level in a cabin with Seapak installed was reduced to 72 decibels and at a cruising speed of 90 mph, the noise level in the passenger cabin of the DC-1 would, on average, be only 65 decibels. To tackle the problems of heating and ventilation—so ineffective in the Ford and Fokker—Raymond tried many possible approaches before settling on the relative efficiency and safety of thermostatically controlled steam heat provided by a small steel boiler in contact with the engine exhaust. For cool air each passenger was served by a self-adjusting air inlet next to his or her seat, the air fed to these inlets through air ducts linked to a

or exceeded most of TWA's requirements.

July 1st 1933. At 12:36 p.m. Douglas chief test pilot Carl Cover flew the new DC-1 from the Clover Field, Santa Monica runway to the cheers and applause of the company employees, most of whom were on their lunch break and able to witness the textbook-perfect take-off.

Then, at a height of less than 100 feet, the left engine coughed and quit. Seconds later the other engine quit. To Arthur Raymond, Donald Douglas, and the others watching their baby descend towards the Pacific Ocean, tragedy seemed inevitable. In the silence of the cockpit, Cover and his co-pilot, Fred

Herman, were seconds from disaster. The experienced pilot pressed the control column forward to gain a little precious airspeed and as he did so both engines suddenly cut in again. Nursing the big plane into a gentle, shallow climb towards 1,000 feet, Cover was now able to think about the problem that faced him, for the first time since the incident began. He knew that his priority was to land the plane immediately while minimizing the risk to the valuable aircraft, his co-pilot and himself. The entire flight lasted twelve minutes. Cover managed to bring the DC-1 around in a somewhat ragged but steady approach back into Clover Field, saving the aeroplane,

WITH A CAPACITY OF FOUR-
TEEN PASSENGERS, THE DC-2
WAS STYLISH AND FAR MORE
COMFORTABLE THAN OTHER
AIRLINERS OF THE TIME. IT
FIRST CARRIED PASSENGERS
OF TWA FROM COLUMBUS,
OHIO, TO NEWARK, NEW
JERSEY ON MAY 14TH 1934.

themselves, and the day for Douglas.

The Douglas engineers were puzzled by the incident. There seemed to be nothing wrong with the engines. Contaminated fuel was suspected. Douglas kept his mechanics and engineers on the investigation around the clock for nearly a week as they thoroughly examined every system of the aircraft. Ground-testing the engines for hours produced no failures. Despite the objections of Wright engineers involved in the search for the cause of the trouble, Carl Cover prevailed in his insistence that the carburettors be examined. The Wright technicians had other ideas about the cause of the problem, but when the new-type carburettors were inspected it was discovered they had been installed backwards. When the plane had climbed out in its take-off and Cover pulled the nose up, the carburettor floats cut the fuel flow to the engines. Simply turning and remounting the carburettors 180 degrees resolved the matter. A second test flight was made a week later and the engines functioned flawlessly, but this time a new problem arose as the pilot felt the big plane "fish-tail" through the air like a swimming shark.

Ozzy Oswald was sent to take a ride in the DC-1 to evaluate the cause of the instability. He and engineer Eugene Root rode in the rear of the plane during the brief flight. Root, "It was like being on the 'Crack-the-Whip' ride at a carnival." The pair fixed the problem by flattening the sides of the rudder, extending its surface area, and adjusting the rudder linkage, all of which resulted in complete stability thereafter.

The DC-1 became the most thoroughly-tested aircraft of the time in over 200 hours of flight and static testing. Emphasis was placed on general performance, speed, stability, structural strength, engines, propeller pitch, and operation in all types of weather conditions.

The next event of importance in the career of the aeroplane came on September 12th at Winslow, Arizona. The agreement with TWA called for the DC-1 to fly and pass a single-engine test flight, either from Los Angeles eastward, or from Winslow westward, on a course over the highest mountains of TWA's routes. Winslow was selected as the starting point because the 4,200-foot altitude and the 100 degree daytime temperature offered the greater challenge in the test. The flight crew consisted of test pilot Eddie Allen, who in 1943 would die testing the B-29 bomber for Boeing, TWA co-pilot Tommy Tomlinson, Douglas engineer Frank Collbohm, and Ozzy Oswald. The aero-

IMPERIAL AIRWAYS LINER "HORATIUS": "HERACLES" CLASS

AIR FRANCE: WIBAULT-PENHOËT 282-T-12.

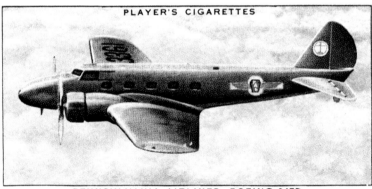

PENNSYLVANIA AIRLINES: BOEING 247D

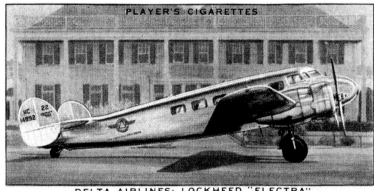

DELTA AIRLINES: LOCKHEED "ELECTRA"

plane was loaded with water ballast bringing the gross weight up to 18,000 pounds. The test began after the take-off roll when the DC-1 left the runway and began to climb. Allen called "Gear up!" and simultaneously reached over and shut down the right engine. To watchers on the ground, the airliner seemed to sag slightly and the propellers appeared barely to clear the runway surface as the plane began to climb again.

Exceeding the requirement of the client, Allen had closed the throttle, shutting down the right-side engine at the most dangerous and critical instant in the take-off, with the wheels still partially down and marginal lift from the wing. Such was his confidence in both the engines and the calculations of his old friend Ozzy Oswald. Oswald, "When Allen cut the engine, he put the operating engine downward and the fuselage straight forward. It was much more efficient to get the side force on the wing. Eddie knew all those things. He was an engineer's dream."

Climbing up to the required 8,000-foot altitude, Allen flew the single-engine test at 130 mph, crossed the Continental Divide and landed on one engine at Albequerque, New Mexico, after a two-hour flight. TWA accepted the DC-1 into its fleet and the age of the tri-motors was at an end.

The DC-1 served for a few years with TWA as a laboratory, flying passengers on the routes of the airline and conducting high-altitude research using advanced supercharged versions of Wright Cyclone engines. Aviator Howard Hughes, who happened to be the largest shareholder in TWA, bought the DC-1 from the airline, intending to attempt a round-the-world record in the plane, but changed his mind and used a Lockheed 14 instead. An Englishman named Forbes then acquired it but soon sold it off to an aircraft broker in France. The aeroplane next appeared in Spanish registration. In December 1940, the DC-1 lost power while taking off from Malaga Airport and crash-landed with severe damage to the airframe. All of the passengers and crew survived. The wreck was soon stripped for spare parts by Spanish Air Force mechanics and what remained was left to rot on the field.

TWA had been so impressed by the DC-1 that they ordered twenty more of the type, but with a number of additional comfort and performance enhancements which, collectively, led to a substantial redesign of the entire airframe. It grew two feet in length, allowing for one more row of seats. The many changes to the overall design brought about a new designation for the resulting airliner, DC-2.

Having absorbed a heavy research and development charge on the DC-1, Douglas was determined to break into profit as soon as possible on the new plane. TWA agreed to a unit price (without engines) of $65,000 and the way seemed clear for Douglas to be in profit on the DC-2 within a reasonable period.

Trans World began taking delivery of the DC-2s early in 1934 and had the first one in scheduled service on May 14th. Just as the DC-1 had put the Ford and the Fokker on the shelf, the DC-2 ended the career of the Boeing 247. So popular was the new Douglas airliner with passengers, that orders for it came flooding in to the Santa Monica plane maker from American Airlines, Eastern Airlines and Pan American Airways. Interest in Europe was aroused as well and the Dutch airline KLM, Europe's oldest airline, soon placed an order for twenty of the new planes.

United Airlines, which for years had been the main competition for TWA, now scrambled desperately to regain its former market share from Trans World. It invested more than a million dollars upgrading its Boeing 247 fleet, but to no avail. The DC-2 was faster, quieter, more comfortable and, in virtually every respect, superior to the Boeing plane.

In October 1934, the MacRobertson London to Melbourne Air Race was staged with a prize of $75,000 cash and a $2,000 gold trophy. The twenty-two entries included a Boeing 247, a Gee Bee racer, and a DC-2 entered by the airline KLM, as well as three specially-built twin-engined De Havilland Comet racers. Most aviation people believed that one of the Comets would run away with the prize and gave no serious consideration to the other entrants. In fact, one of the Comets did win the 11,300-mile race, in a time of seventy hours fifty-four minutes. The second fastest finisher, to the astonishment of nearly everyone, was the DC-2, which landed just thirty-four minutes after the Comet. The KLM airliner made the flight over its existing route, adding an extra thousand miles to the trip. It also carried three passengers, a navigator, a mechanic, the pilot and co-pilot, and more than 400 pounds of mail. The achievement added enormously to the growing reputation of Douglas and the DC-2 and within six months of the DC-2's introduction, Douglas had seventy-five firm orders for the plane.

An article in the July 1934 edition of *Scientific American* stated:

"The DC-2 put American commercial aviation years ahead of Europe. The airlines, faced with decreasing revenues from the mails and with competition from the railroads, showed great wisdom in not merely stepping up the speed of their service. With the DC-2 they made conscious efforts to make every air trip comfortable for the passenger. When a traveller boarded the plane, a friendly flight attendant, or co-pilot, handed the passenger a little package containing chewing gum, and cotton for his ears. With the improvement in noise elimination in the DC-2 the cotton soon became an artifact."

A year after publication of this article, the DC-2 was being operated by twenty European airlines. Three of the planes, in the fleet of the Spanish airline Lineas Aeroeas Postales Espanolas, became the first Douglas commercial transports to go to war. The Spanish DC-2s were converted to bombers after serving briefly in the Spanish Civil War beginning in 1936. Presaging what was to come with C-47s many years later in the Vietnam War, the DC-2 "bombers" were fitted with machine-guns in the last two windows of the cabin, with a third gun mounted in the roof behind the cockpit. An internal bomb rack led to the rear doorway where a crewman tossed the small bombs out by hand.

Another strange acquisition of the DC-2 occurred when the Soviets purchased a single example, which they then copied without license or permission. They designated the result ANT-35 and powered it with Rhone-Gnome engines. A further example of foreign interest in the DC-2 took place in 1934 when the Nakajima Company of Japan entered negotiations with Douglas to replace its old tri-motor aircraft with DC-2s. In March of that year Nakajima paid $80,000 for the right to build and sell the DC-2 in Japan and Manchuria and began operation in November. The forerunner of Japan Air Lines also bought five unbuilt DC-2 airframes which they assembled and modified with Japanese instrumentation. These aircraft were designated AT-2, later changed to Ki-34, and flew from Fukuoka to Taipei, Formosa. Japanese-built DC-2s entered service in September 1936.

As impressive as it was, the DC-2 was not without problems. The author and pilot Ernest K. Gann wrote: "There are two kinds of airplanes. Those you fly, and those that fly you. With the DC-2 you must have the distinct understanding at the very start who is the boss . . . you will learn to love this airplane; and you will also learn to hate it. When taxiing, the braking system in the DC-2 was activated by a heavy horn-shaped han-

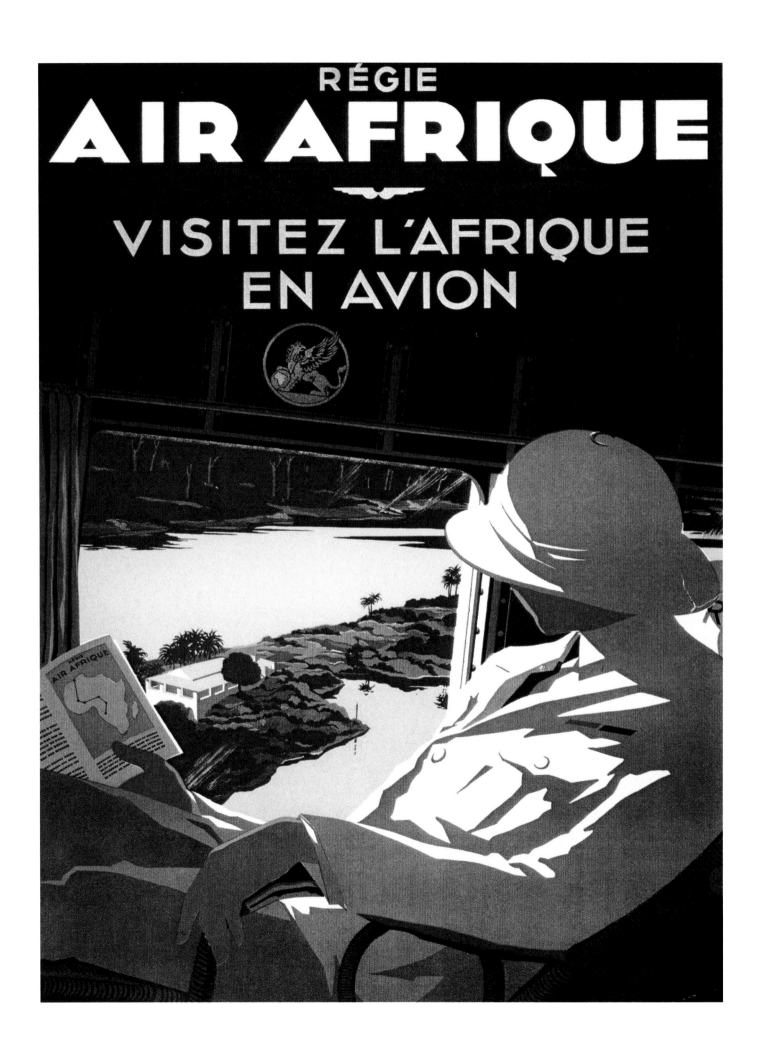

dle protruding from the left side of the instrument panel. By simultaneous use of the rudder and handle, the desired left brake and right brake could be applied. Since there was an inevitable lag between motion and effect, the DC-2 was stubbornly determined to chase its own tail on the ground, and in the crosswinds, sometimes switching ends to the embarrassment of all aboard.

"The air is annoyingly potted with a multitude of minor vertical disturbances that sicken the passengers, and keep us captives of our seat belts. We sweat in the cockpit, although much of the time we fly with the side windows open. The airplane smells of hot oil, and simmering aluminum, disinfectant, faeces, leather and puke. The stewardesses, short-tempered and reeking of vomit, come forward as often as they can for what is a breath of comparatively fresh air.

"When flying in the rain, the cockpit windshields leaked so badly the effect within was that of a seriously depth-bombed submarine.

"The steam heat system, centralized about a boiler in the forward baggage compartment, was alleged to have been designed by Machiavelli. Much of the time the contraption gagged, gurgled and regurgitated ominously, and to the dismay of the passengers occasionally filled the entire interior of the aircraft with vapors."

As good and sound as the DC-2 was, neither it nor its record of flight safety was perfect. 20,000,000 miles of safe flying in twenty-one countries notwithstanding, bad things could and did happen to the aircraft and its passengers. In foul weather during a flight from Los Angeles to Kansas City in 1934, TWA 323 contacted the Kansas City tower for landing instructions and was told that the field was closed due to the weather. The tower personnel instructed the captain to proceed to an emergency airfield 130 miles away. Arriving over the emergency field, the captain found it to be socked-in with solid cloud cover but, with no remaining fuel reserve, elected to descend and try to land. Sadly, his angle of descent was too great and the plane slammed through a fence and narrowly missed a farmhouse. While eleven of the twelve passengers survived the crash-landing, the pilot, co-pilot, flight attendant and one passenger did not. The unfortunate passenger was U.S. Senator Bronson Cutting—the first fatality for TWA since the crash that had killed football coach Knute Rockne. Cutting's death brought a Senate investigation and what some have termed a "head-hunting expedition"

against the airlines, with TWA singled out for particular attention. The press had a field day with the story and the reputations of Douglas Aircraft and the DC-2 were not spared. In the end though, the report of the official investigation into the crash blamed it on the bad weather in the area and the inadequacy of the weather reporting. The pilots, the aircraft and its designers were cleared of any culpability in the incident and the solid reputation of Douglas for building sound and structurally reliable aircraft was intact.

On the DC-2, the famed aviation pioneer Igor Sikorsky was quoted, "American aviation is definitely superior to European aviation. I think the only airplanes of this size being built in Germany are the Junkers three-engine transports. These ships, although excellent in themselves, do not attain the performance of the DC-2."

The popularity and impact of the DC-2 was unprecedented. By the end of its production a total of 193 DC-2s had been sold and delivered to the airline and military customers of Douglas Aircraft, resulting in a significant profit for the company.

Many years after the development of the DC-1 and DC-2, Arthur Raymond commented, "The most important contribution of the DC-2 to aviation technology was its bridge to the DC-3."

LEGEND

In July 1936, U.S. President Franklin D. Roosevelt awarded Donald W. Douglas the Collier Trophy—aviation's highest honour—for the design and development of the DC-2, forerunner of the legendary DC-3. The President said: "The airplane, by reason of its high speed, economy, and quiet passenger comfort has been generally adopted by transport lines throughout the United States. Its merit has been further recognized by its adoption abroad and its influence on foreign design is already apparent."

"Probably the most memorable thing about the Dakota was the smell. The odour of the leather mixed with hydraulic fluid made a perfume second to none. The plane always treated me well, unlike some of the other birds I've flown, and my memories of it are all good."
– Tex Gehman, Winnipeg, Canada

Like the Spitfire, Mustang, and a small number of other classic aircraft, the DC-3/Dakota is a breed apart, distinguished not only by her lovely shape and exceptional design, engineering, durability and performance, as well as other fine qualities and characteristics, but by her enormous base of admirers. From the millions of people who have been her passengers, to the enthusiastic captains and crews who have operated her for more than seventy years, to her countless fans in the aviation world, and those whose lives have been affected by her in the most dramatic ways, she is truly unforgettable.

"We hauled GIs and admirals, ammunition, parts for tanks and submarines, medical equipment, engines, machine-guns, fighter pilots, prisoners-of-war and Indian troopers, jerked beef, land mines, tires, beer, entire P-40s with their wings slung below the fuselage and everything else inside, gold bars and jeeps, and tractors, statesmen, war correspondents, USO entertainers, horses, mysterious men in civilian attire who did not say who they were, wounded infantrymen and plasma and a lot of other things, usual and odd, that have a part in the waging of desert war. If it could be torn down into pieces that fit through a C-47's cargo doors and didn't bring the gross weight to more than 27,500 pounds, we hauled it. If it ran the weight up an extra 1,000 or so pounds, we falsified the load sheets and went anyway."
– A World War Two C-47 pilot

During the mid-1930s three airlines, TWA, United Airlines, and American Airlines offered trans-continental passenger service in the United States. Of the three, only American provided sleeper service initially. The aircraft it operated on the route was the slow but relatively comfortable Curtiss Condor II biplane, but by 1935 it was clear to Cyrus Smith, president of American, that since the introduction of the greatly superior Douglas DC-2 into airline service, the days of his Condor were numbered. Smith needed help fast and, like TWA's Jack Frye before him, he contacted Donald Douglas. Unlike Frye who had written a letter, Smith telephoned Douglas and in a two-hour, $300 call, managed to persuade the California plane maker to modify ten DC-2s for American to operate as "sleepers." Initially, Douglas was not enthusiastic about Smith's request for a new airliner that would be larger and more comfortable than the Condor and better than both the Boeing 247 and the DC-2. Production of the DC-2 was in full stride with more than 100 of the planes delivered and a further ninety on the order books. The massive work involved in design, re-tooling and manufacturing a new model for Smith seemed to Donald Douglas a headache he didn't need, and Douglas was unconvinced by Smith's business commitment to night flying and the sleeper service. But Smith persisted and by the end of the conversation he had obtained agreement from Douglas to modify the ten DC-2s that American had already ordered.

It is believed that the actual idea for modifying the DC-2 to a sleeper had come about in a conversation between C.R. Smith and his chief engineer, William Littlewood, as the two were boarding a flight from Dallas to Los Angeles in the summer of 1934. Smith is supposed to have said, "Bill, what we need is a DC-2 sleeper plane!" When he returned to American's Chicago headquarters, Littlewood involved his assistant, Otto Kirchner, in the development of detailed ideas for what would range well beyond mere minor changes in the DC-2. They included more powerful Wright Cyclone engines to cope with the increased gross weight of the new plane, and a wider fuselage to accommodate either fourteen sleeping berths or twenty-one seats for day-passengers, as well as an appropriate aisle. They estimated an 85 percent parts commonality with the DC-2 for their new stretched sleeper.

As the Douglas engineers got down to designing the sleeper for American, it became obvious that they were faced with a

brand new aeroplane, not a minor modification of their highly successful DC-2. At a time when they struggled to keep pace with the world-wide demand for DC-2, they had little capacity for the sleeper project. Fortunately, many of the design calculations had already been made by engineers of American Airlines.

Even so, with no airline other than American showing any interest in sleeper planes, Donald Douglas was reluctant to devote much of the company's facilities to a small order for a very specialized model. What did inspire him to cooperate with C.R. Smith was the possibility (if only a remote one) of a new

SEE AMERICA BY AIR
SUGGESTED AIRPLANE TOURS
of the UNITED STATES and MEXICO

and far wider market for the basic aeroplane that would result from the redesign for American. With a fuselage two and a half feet longer and twenty-six inches wider, and a proper aisle, the new model would accommodate twenty-one day passengers and might attract the interest of other airlines. What may have clinched the deal for Douglas was Smith's assurance that he could get $4,500,000 in loan funding from the government to finance the purchase of up to twenty of the new models, the first ten of which would be sleepers. Smith agreed to pay $79,500 each for the new planes (less engines and other items that the airline would provide). This was all agreed in that late-1934 phone call to Douglas and, in December 1935, the first Douglas Sleeper Transport or DST was rolled out of the Santa Monica factory. The day-passenger version would be designated DC-3.

Nearly twenty years after the DC-3 first flew, Douglas introduced Smith as the featured speaker at a dinner. "This is an ideal time to acknowledge our debt of gratitude to my good friend C.R. Smith for his part in the development of the DC-3. He had tremendous faith in us, and in the future of air travel. His boundless energy, clear vision, and uncanny knack in making the right decision at the right time were the catalytic agents that greatly influenced us in taking steps to build that famous aeroplane."

As design work on the DST progressed, it was clear to the Douglas engineers and to Donald Douglas that the original estimate of an 85 percent parts commonality had been wildly inaccurate. Both Littlewood and Smith, having done some research of their own while flying in DC-2s, had had a number of concerns about that aircraft. These added substantially to the design requirement while significantly reducing the parts commonality of the DST and DC-2. They included insufficient power, heavy aileron and rudder control, reported directional instability, excessive yawing in turbulence, and propeller and fin icing problems. All of these deficiencies led Littlewood to press for what amounted to a virtually new design. To a great extent, it was the friendly, cooperative working relationship between Bill Littlewood, Otto Kirchner, and Arthur Raymond of Douglas, that allowed the critical six-month design phase of the DST programme to be accomplished with a minimum of friction.

The work on the DST at Santa Monica was also advanced through the assistance of American Airlines which provided one of their Curtiss Condor airliners for the Douglas engineers to evaluate in planning improved sleeping berths. Littlewood and Douglas's Harry Wetzel devoted many hours to the task. A highly-detailed mock-up was built to help in identifying and resolving potential problems, such as passenger claustrophobia in the upper berths (dealt with through the installation of small additional windows). Raymond, ". . . we spent more than half our time in the shop [on the DST project] and we had over 400 engineers and draftsmen working on the design. We spent many long nights producing more than 3,500 drawings, but it was worth it." Thus did the approach and perspective of the Douglas team evolve over the course of their work on the DST/DC-3.

Raymond: "The DC-3 was almost a new airplane as far as actual parts, but it was two-thirds finished before we started because we were so far ahead (in design and development) with work on the DC-2." The rollout of the first Douglas American Skysleeper took place on December 14th 1935—the emergence of an aeroplane quite different from its DC-2 forebear. The DST was longer, wider, had a larger tail fin, a wider wingspan, beefed-up landing gear, and more powerful engines. In terms of spare parts commonality with the DC-2, only about 10 percent were interchangeable.

With the introduction of the DST and the DC-3 that followed it, air travellers would experience an entirely new level of comfort, convenience and safety on their journeys. To distinguish the interior from those of earlier and existing airliners, Douglas deliberately avoided the use of certain greens and other colours believed to affect passengers negatively with balance and airsickness problems. The interiors were done in light, airy colours to appear more spacious; the carpeting was dark to give a feeling of security. Again, Dr Stephen Zand was given the challenge of soundproofing the passenger cabin and managed to insulate it to a sound level of only fifty-five decibels, similar to that of a railway carriage of the time. Air conditioning and heating systems were based on the lessons learned in the development of the DC-2, as were other systems pioneered on the DC-1 and DC-2. The landing gear, for example, was stronger than that of its predecessors, with better shock absorbers and engine-driven hydraulic oil pumps that raised and lowered the gear in seven seconds, as opposed to the sixty or more seconds required by the hand-pump system of the DC-2.

The stable, comfortable ride and easy control of the DST/DC-3 did not happen through luck or good fortune. The airframe was larger and different in many important respects from that of the DC-2. Ozzy Oswald, "We tried dozens of models in the wind tunnel before we hit on the secret. We narrowed the airfoil, which changed the centre of balance of the airplane. The final wing design was enormously strong." Additionally, the Douglas engineers reinforced the wing top skin with span-wise corrugated sheeting, making the wing stronger and better able to withstand compression. The wings also had a certain amount of built-in flexibility, allowing them to "flap" up to five degrees in flight, a slightly disconcerting characteristic when first observed by some passengers. They were reassured by the captain or a flight crew member that the phenomenon was normal. This was, after all, the first important commercial airliner constructed without struts or wires on the wings—a novelty for most travellers. Another innovation was the wing-mounted leading-edge lights used instead of the nose-mounted lights of the DC-2. The repositioning brought improved visibility for the pilots in poor weather conditions.

Among the more impressive advances employed in the DST/DC-3 was the latest version of automatic variable propeller pitch which eased all aspects of engine performance, from take-off, through climb-out, cruise, descent and landing. This, in combination with new, hydraulically operated trailing edge wing flaps, greatly improved both the lift of the wing on take-off and the ability to bleed off airspeed on the landing approach for a slower, safer, more comfortable landing.

Historians disagree about why Donald Douglas, most of his personnel and the media seemed to take little interest in the first flight of the DST/DC-3. The take-off started the career of what may be the most important aircraft ever built, and was among the most significant events of the twentieth century. Yet, only a handful of engineers and draftsmen turned out on that sunny afternoon of December 17th 1935 to watch the shiny new airliner turn onto the Clover Field runway and begin its take-off roll. Carl Cover was again at the controls, but there would be no repeat of the near-disaster that had occurred on the maiden flight of the DC-1 in July 1933. In fact, years later, the principals of the company recalled that the day and the event itself were so routine that none of the Douglas executives took time out to witness it. Carl Cover, "I remember nothing beyond that it took place on that day. It was unremarkable—just another routine flight, similar to hundreds of others." Frank Collbohm, "I don't even remember whether it happened in the morning or afternoon. I can't separate it in my mind from any of the other test flights we made in those days. Obviously, everything was fine. There was nothing special; it was just another airplane going up." And Arthur Raymond recalled, "When the airplane was ready, Carl and the others simply got aboard and took off. Of course, none of us had any idea it marked the start of an era." Perhaps the most historically staggering realization about the event is that, as far as is known, it was not even photographed. Research has failed to turn up a single photo of the flight. The event passed practically unrecorded.

Decades after that first flight of the DST/DC-3, Arthur Raymond said that he had been asked again and again if he and the others in charge at Douglas had had any idea that the aeroplane would last fifty years. "Of course we didn't! Our biggest decision was the question of whether to design the fuselage tooling for twenty-five airplanes or fifty. We took a deep breath and we said let's go for fifty. Off that tooling we built 300. We made another set of tooling, three plants, and the rest is history. We didn't have any idea what was evolving. Looking back, we were right to be conservative. We didn't know we were building a legend."

Executives of other airlines, who had previously yawned when the subject of sleeper service came up, were suddenly alert, interested and demanding a piece of that particular action. The advantage that American Airlines had secured with its order for the first lot of DSTs found them suddenly clamouring for their own sleeper planes and rushing to place orders with Douglas. They all watched jealously as American launched its inaugural Flagship service with the new planes, from Newark to Chicago on June 26th 1936. The DST made the flight in just three hours and fifty-five minutes, against eighteen hours by train. On September 18th, American began the first coast-to-coast Flagship sleeper service and, in that same month, began taking delivery of the first DC-3 day-passenger planes from the Santa Monica plant. A few months later, American started its DC-3 Mercury Service, flying from New York to California in fifteen hours—impressive to travellers who had been enduring a thirty-three hour trip in the Ford and Fokker Tri-Motor planes that made twenty-five or more stops en route and required some night-time travel by train.

The adventure for the early passengers aboard the American DST included hot meals served in-flight by a stewardess. Gone were sandwich-and-an-apple box lunches, to be replaced by service on china with quality silverware. Breakfasts offered pancakes or omelettes; lunches were often soup, fried chicken and vegetables with ice cream for dessert, and dinners included steaks, Long Island duckling, or Chicken Kiev, with salad and dessert. For twenty-one passengers, the meal service normally took about an hour.

With an eye towards the business executive who wanted and was willing to pay for a higher level of comfort and pampering on routes such as New York-Chicago, United Airlines offered "Club" service on its DC-3 Sky Lounge Mainliners, specially fitted with only fourteen seats—overstuffed lounge chairs that could be rotated at the press of a button to face a window or across the aisle or towards the rear of the plane. By June 1st 1937, American, United, and TWA were all offering a transcontinental DST sleeper service.

Up in the cockpit, flying and working conditions for the pilots were also greatly improved over those in the previous generation of airliners. A perfect operating environment had still to be achieved, however. The windshield of the DST/DC-3, for example, leaked in a storm, causing some captains and co-pilots to wear rubber aprons. Years later, with the advent of common silicone sealants, the problem was finally resolved.

With the arrival in the airline industry of the DC-3, it was clear at Douglas that the formerly bulging order book for the DC-2 would soon have to make way for burgeoning DC-3 production. Ironically, in their planning and calculations for the DST, Bill Littlewood and Otto Kirchner had laid much of the foundation for the coming DC-3 and had accelerated the end of production for the DST. They used the new Wright 1,000 hp Cyclone engines on the sleeper and, with the additional power, believed they could increase the lifting capacity of the plane and improve its profitability. In juggling the seating and baggage arrangement, they were able to seat twenty-one passengers for a fifty percent payload increase over that of the DC-2; this with only a three percent operating cost increase. The economic balance now tipped heavily in favour of the DC-3 day-plane version over the DST. The new, more powerful engines easily coped with the passenger and baggage weight increase and the DST's fate was

A FORMATION OF AMERICAN AIRLINES DC-3S OVER NEW YORK CITY IN THE LATE '30S

VERLAAGD TARIEF NAAR NEDERLAND
20 CENT PER 10 GRAM

HET VERHEUGDE INDIË

EERSTE VLUCHT PER DC-3
(DOUGLAS C-3)

PER LUCHTPOST PAR AVION

Een nieuwe dag is opgestaan

. . . .
. . . .

Hoor, hoe de morgenklokken
luiden,
Hoe ze luiden
den nieuwen dageraad.
P. C. BOUTENS

AAN *Mevrouw M. A. E. van Loghem.*

Prins Mauritslaan 22

Holland   's Gravenhage

VISSER

LEGER DES HEILS-WELDADIGHEIDSPOSTZEGELS TEN BATE v/h INDISCHE KIND

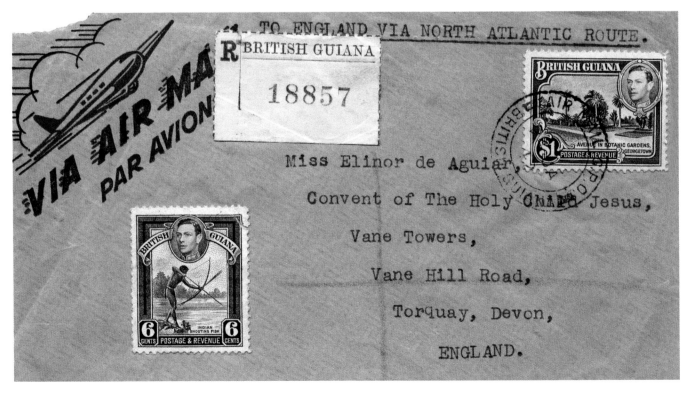

TO ENGLAND VIA NORTH ATLANTIC ROUTE.

R BRITISH GUIANA
18857

Miss Elinor de Aguiar,

Convent of The Holy Child Jesus,

Vane Towers,

Vane Hill Road,

Torquay, Devon,

ENGLAND.

CHRISTMAS EVE 1946. A C-53 (DC-3) OF WESTERN AIRLINES, FLIGHT 44, DEPARTED FROM HOLTVILLE, CALIFORNIA, AT 6:50 PM, EN ROUTE TO SAN DIEGO. IT HAD BEEN CLEARED TO FLY UNDER VISUAL FLIGHT RULES AT 7,000 FEET. AT 7:09 THE PILOT CONTACTED LOS ANGELES DISPATCHER AND REPORTED HIS POSITION AS "OVER MT LAGUNA" ABOUT 60 MILES EAST OF SAN DIEGO. HE THEN SWITCHED TO THE SAN DIEGO LINDBERGH FIELD TOWER RADIO FREQUENCY AND CONTACTED THE MT LAGUNA CHECKPOINT OPERATOR, WISHING HIM A MERRY CHRISTMAS. THE OPERATOR PROVIDED A LOCAL WEATHER REPORT WHICH THE PILOT ACKNOWLEDGED. AT 7:18 HE WAS HEARD ATTEMPTING TO CONTACT LINDBERGH TOWER. THE TOWER RADIO OPERATOR RESPONDED BUT THERE WAS NO FURTHER CONTACT WITH THE AIRCRAFT. WHEN THE AIRCRAFT BECAME OVERDUE AT LINDBERGH FIELD, A SEARCH WAS INITIATED BUT THE WEATHER DETERIORATED AND NO FURTHER AIR SEARCH WAS POSSIBLE FOR SEVERAL DAYS. FRIDAY DECEMBER 27. A GROUND SEARCH PARTY IN EASTERN SAN DIEGO COUNTY DISCOVERED THE BURNT AND SCATTERED WRECKAGE OF WESTERN FLIGHT 44 SOUTH AND EAST OF MT LAGUNA ON CUYAPAIPE MOUNTAIN AT THE 6,100-FOOT LEVEL. ALL TWELVE ABOARD THE PLANE HAD DIED IN THE CRASH. THE PILOT'S LAST POSITION REPORT HAD BEEN INCORRECT. AN ACCIDENT INVESTIGATOR'S THEORY IS THAT THE PILOT HAD SEEN AND MISTAKEN AN ILLUMINATED NAVIGATIONAL BEACON EAST OF THE LAGUNA RANGE, FOR ONE HE KNEW TO BE LOCATED ON MT LAGUNA. ANOTHER CRITICAL FACTOR WAS THAT THE FLIGHT HAD BEEN IMPROPERLY CLEARED TO FLY AT AN ALTITUDE OF 7,000 FEET WHEN CIVIL AIR REGULATIONS REQUIRED "1,000 FEET OF CLEARANCE ABOVE TERRAIN". THE

CONTINUED ON PAGE 57

sealed. Airline customers could order even more powerful twin-row fourteen cylinder Pratt & Whitney R-1830 Twin Wasp engines, each of which generated up to 1,200 hp. Only forty of the sleeper planes would ever be built, as the airlines quickly moved to take full advantage of the greater earning potential in the DC-3. The new airliner came with many other advantages as well. Its style of construction made it easy to maintain and repair. The wings and vertical fin could be fitted with de-icer boots housing flexible tubes which, when inflated with compressed air, expanded and cracked accumulated ice from the leading-edge surfaces.

The DST came with two lavatories, one for men and one for women, both located at the rear of the cabin. The buffet area was at the front of the cabin, while on the DC-3 both galley and the single lavatory were located at the rear. Passenger seat positions were fitted with individual adjustable cool air ducts, a reading light and a cabin attendant call switch. Of all the features provided on the DST/DC-3, only one was almost universally unpopular with passengers—the steam-generated cabin heating system. Early travellers complained that it kept the cabin too hot or too cold, that it leaked and that it frequently malfunctioned. In time, Douglas solved the problem by fitting a "muff" around the engine exhausts that heated ram air ducted into the cabin.

Ample, well-located access panels in the fuselage and wings simplified the work of airline mechanics, and such routine jobs as changing an engine could now be accomplished by three mechanics in only two hours, reducing costly maintenance delays and keeping the planes flying and earning for more hours of the day and night. The DC-3 was normally equipped with ample overhead storage for carry-on or hand luggage. Mail and baggage were stowed in a forward compartment located just behind the cockpit and loaded through the small door on the left side of the nose. A rear baggage compartment aft of the lavatory was loaded through another left-side door. Schedule efficiency, performance and safety were improving as well, and the unit cost to the airlines was still attractive, especially when purchased in quantity at a significant discount. The original list price for a DST or DC-3 was between $90,000 and $110,000 in 1936, topping at around $115,000 by 1939—all dependent on equipment ordered by the customer, the amount of training requested by customer flight and maintenance personnel and after-delivery factory support.

It was the powerful economic advantage afforded to those airlines equipped with the DC-3, that guaranteed its success for them and for Douglas. American's C.R. Smith, "The DC-3 freed the airlines from complete dependence upon government mail pay. It was an airplane that could make money by just handling passengers. With previous planes, if you multiplied the number of seats by the fares you couldn't break even, not even with 100 percent load." The chief engineer for the C-53 (one of the military versions of the DC-3), Malcolm Oleson, "It [the DC-3] introduced higher speed, and greater comfort. It was very reliable. The DC-3 gave aviation a sense of security. People suddenly had faith in the airplane. This airplane made the airplane look good to everyone. That is why so many people have a soft spot in their heart for the DC-3; a lot of people had their first air travel in one."

The safety factor would always be of utmost importance to air passengers who, in most cases, did not fly for the thrill of the ride, but to get where they were going quickly and safely. Unfortunately, accidents involving DC-3s claimed the lives of several well-known and celebrated people. Among them was the singer and actress Grace Moore, who died on January 26th 1947 in the crash of a KLM DC-3 shortly after taking off from Copenhagen, on a flight to Stockholm, to continue a concert tour.

Film actor Leslie Howard is probably best remembered for his role as Ashley Wilkes in the 1939 classic *Gone With The Wind*. Howard was killed on June 1st 1943 when the BOAC DC-3 he was travelling in from Lisbon to London was attacked and shot down over the Bay of Biscay by a Junkers Ju 88 of the German Air Force. Various theories have been put forward over the years as to why the Luftwaffe downed the regularly-scheduled civilian airliner, including the largely discredited notion that they had believed British Prime Minister Winston Churchill to have been on board. The more generally accepted theory is that Howard himself was their target, as they believed him to be spying for Britain while in the guise of an entertainer on a goodwill tour. A possible further German motivation might have been to demoralize the British people in time of war through the loss of one of their most famously patriotic celebrities.

The beautiful and talented movie star and comedienne Carole Lombard was one of the best-known and most highly-regarded actresses of the 1920s, 30s and 40s. She was married to the Hollywood idol Clark Gable who, coincidentally, was another star of *Gone With The Wind*. Following America's entry into the Second World War late in 1941, Lombard travelled to Indiana to appear in a bond rally, raising money for the American war effort. Together with her mother, she boarded a TWA DC-3 to return to Los Angeles on the morning of January 16th 1942. The aircraft landed at Las Vegas to refuel. It then took off in a clear evening sky but reportedly went off-course, owing to the wartime blackout of aircraft beacons in the area. Twenty-three minutes after leaving Las Vegas the plane slammed into Double-Up Peak on Mount Potosi. There were no survivors. For her war bond fund-raising efforts, President Franklin Roosevelt declared Lombard the first American woman to be killed during the war in the line of duty and awarded her the Presidential Medal of Freedom. She was thirty-three. The inconsolable Gable then joined the U.S. Army Air Forces and flew several bombing missions as a B-17 gunner from a base in England.

In 1937 the first examples of what would become known as "black boxes" were installed in the DC-3s of United Airlines. Also known as Flight Analysers, the devices recorded the aircraft's altitude, rate of climb and descent, and when the autopilot was operating and when radio transmission took place. In the event of an accident, they aided investigators in finding the cause. United's pilots were initially hostile when the devices were adopted, perceiving them as "spies in the sky" and "flying stool pigeons." Despite their initial objections, however, the black box concept evolved over time into the more sophisticated and vitally important system now used in all commercial aircraft.

In general, with most airlines flying DC-3 equipment by 1938, leading carriers like American, United, TWA, Eastern, and Continental, were building up excellent safety records. American, for example, was awarded a National Safety Council citation for having flown more than 410,338,000 passenger-miles without a passenger fatality by that year.

Domestic airlines purchasing DC-3s or DSTs were not only glad to have them, they also appreciated the ease in taking delivery by simply sending a company crew to fly their new plane from the Douglas factory ramp in Santa Monica to their home field. The delivery process was more difficult for foreign customers since the plane did not have trans-oceanic range and had to be delivered by ship as deck cargo. This entailed anti-salt water

protection, sealing the airframes with coatings of grease or cosmoline, which added to the overall cost of the purchase. Alternatively, the overseas customer could opt for the aircraft to be delivered by air after installation of temporary additional fuel tanks, and this operation would become the norm following wartime establishment of the North Atlantic Ferry Route for flying American war planes to Europe. After the United States entered the Second World War in December 1941, the ferry flights of DC-3s began. One result was that several examples came into the possession of the Nazis—the earliest such incidents arising with the German invasions of Holland and Belgium in 1940. And, early in 1939, the Germans had confiscated several DC-2s and DC-3s in Czechoslovakia when they annexed that country. For a while the Luftwaffe was operating more of the Douglas airliners than the U.S. Army, which had very few of the planes in its inventory at that time.

While no one at Douglas had an inkling of the actual production numbers they would be dealing with over the coming years, they were beginning to understand the impact that the DC-3 was having upon the airlines of the world. Until the advent of the DC-2, American-designed and manufactured airliners had attracted little interest in the world marketplace. With the coming of the DC-3, virtually all other airliner types became obsolete. Most of world airliner sales post-1935 until World War II were made by Douglas Aircraft and most of them were DC-3s. The age of American domination of the airliner market had begun in earnest and, until the formation of the Airbus aircraft consortium in 1970, it continued unchallenged.

The DC-3 faced no significant competition during its main years of development and manufacture. Only the Lockheed Aircraft Company's 1940 attempt with its Model 18 Lodestar came anywhere near offering as much. However, the far better range of the Douglas plane ruled out the Lodestar as serious airline competition. Most of the Lodestars produced went to the military, with a number of specialty variants made, such as the Ventura bomber. Curtiss-Wright tried competing against the DC-3 with the 36-passenger twin-engine C-W 20 (also in 1940), which was slightly larger and heavier, and was powered by 1,700 hp twin-row Wright R-2600 Twin Cyclone engines. The plane was never certificated for commercial airline use, although, ultimately, the U.S. Army ordered it as the C-46 Commando.

Due to its shape, some pilots referred to it as "the whale" or the "Curtiss Calamity." 3,140 of the planes were built between 1940 and 1945 and it gained a measure of fame as a principal workhorse flying "The Hump" (the Himalaya mountains), bringing vitally needed supplies to troops in China from India and Burma (see the chapter, AT WAR).

Until the arrival of the DC-3 on the world market, the best selling and most widely flown airliner was the Junkers Ju 52 with 4,835 produced, in Germany, France, and Spain. These slow but sturdy airliners served in large numbers until well into the 1960s, when most were replaced by DC-3s.

Long before the war, Douglas was in the enviable position of having such a big hit on its hands, that the company was unable to keep up with the demand for the DC-3. Consequently, when it received expressions of interest from Japan, Holland, and Russia to manufacture the airplane in their countries under license from the California plane maker, Douglas moved quickly to issue the licenses. Antony Fokker's firm held the Dutch license and continued to act as European distributor for the plane, but never actually built them. The DC-3 civilian airliner was made in quantity by both the Japanese and Russians beginning in 1938. The Japanese programme began with the importation from Santa Monica of nineteen DC-3s and DC-3As, as well as two unassembled airframes to be used in making patterns. Douglas sent design and technical personnel to Japan to assist in getting their production under way, and between 1939 and 1945 some 487 of the aircraft were produced there. Wartime shortages forced the Japanese to make some compromises to the Douglas design, such as substituting wood for fabric on the control surfaces.

The Russians sent their representative, Boris Lisunov, to Santa Monica in 1938 to learn about the Douglas manufacturing procedures in preparation for his country's own programme to build the DC-3. It would be known as the Li-2 (Lisunov) and was to be produced in State Aircraft Plant Number 84 near Moscow. However, the German invasion forced the manufacture to be moved to a new plant in Tashkent near the Afghanistan border. The Russian version of the plane would differ from the Douglas civil airliner design far more than the Japanese product. It had larger cargo doors and, most significantly, a 7.2mm machine-gun was fitted in a power turret at the

7,000-FOOT CLEARANCE HAD BEEN INSUFFICIENT FOR THE LOCAL TERRAIN. FOLLOWING THE CRASH INVESTIGATION, WESTERN AIRLINES REVISED ITS MINIMUM NIGHT CLEARANCE ALTITUDE ON THE RUN TO 9,000 FEET. THE CIVIL AERONAUTICS BOARD REPORT ON THE ACCIDENT CONCLUDED THAT THE PROBABLE CAUSE WAS THAT THE FLIGHT HAD BEEN CONDUCTED "AT AN ALTITUDE WHICH WOULD NOT CLEAR OBSTRUCTIONS, DUE TO AN ERROR BY THE PILOT IN DETERMINING HIS POSITION" WITH RESPECT TO THE MOUNTAINS ON THE PLANE'S FLIGHT PATH. THREE CREW MEMBERS AND NINE PASSENGERS PERISHED IN THE CRASH. THE CRASH SITE OF WESTERN FLIGHT 44 IS SHOWN IN THE PHOTOGRAPH ON PAGES 54-55.

centre of the cabin roof. Some Russian models had bomb racks installed and some were built with side-blister windows for photo-reconnaissance missions. There were also passenger and combined passenger-cargo versions. The primary powerplant used was the 900 hp Shevstov M-62, a Cyclone engine built in Russia under license from Wright. A later version, the Li-3, was powered by American-made Wright Cyclones. In all the Russians built 2,930 of the type.

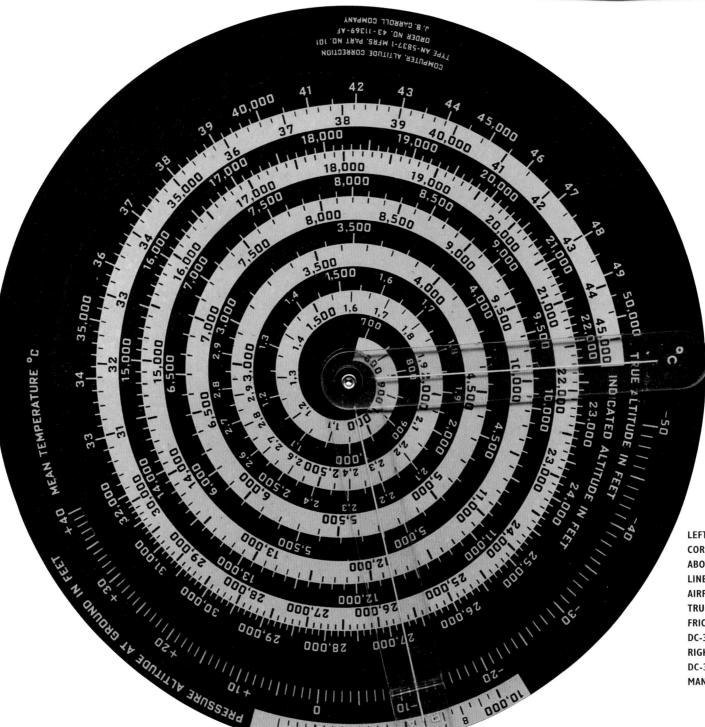

COMPUTER, ALTITUDE CORRECTION
TYPE AN-5837-1 MFRS, PART NO. 101
ORDER NO. 43-11369-AF
J. B. CARROLL COMPANY

LEFT: A CARROLL ALTITUDE
CORRECTION COMPUTER;
ABOVE: AN AMERICAN AIR-
LINES ERTL 1939 DODGE
AIRFLOW FLIGHT SERVICE
TRUCK MODEL; RIGHT: A
FRICTION-POWERED TOY
DC-3 BY SCHYLLING; BELOW
RIGHT: ANOTHER TIN-PLATE
DC-3 TOY OF UNKNOWN
MANUFACTURE.

N1944A

The basic role of the American and British airborne troop carrier organizations in World War II was to bring large formations of aircraft, flying at relatively low levels, to deliver the forward combat soldiers in key Allied invasions, as both paratroopers and gliderborne infantry. No aircraft of the time was better suited to that role than the Douglas C-47/Skytrain/Dakota.

The job of the air crews was demanding and dangerous. Flying unarmed aircraft, they had virtually no means of protecting themselves over enemy-occupied territory. In the beginning, their operations were flown at night, without navigation lights. They struggled to maintain tight formations, mere hundreds of feet from the ground and at very low airspeeds. Their exposure to both enemy flak and small arms fire was so extreme that steel-pot infantry helmets were part of their required flying kit.

Until the final year of the war, the pilots had to rely on dead-reckoning and the crude, often unreliable navigation technology of the day, with minimal ground-to-air communications to assist them. Locating and reaching the drop and landing zones could range from the difficult to the nearly impossible. In many cases, the airborne and glider troops landed well away from their prescribed destinations, widely scattered and sometimes hopelessly separated from each other, their units, and their commanders. As with some bomber crews in the Royal Air Force of WWII, a few troop carrier pilots were accused, rightly or wrongly, of what was then called "creep-back", a proclivity for dropping their paratroopers or releasing their gliders early, short of the target, in order to depart the danger zone sooner and possibly improve their chances of surviving the trip. The pilots were frequently facing combat for the first time and some were as frightened and apprehensive as most or all of their passengers. Like the paratroopers, however, most of them accepted the odds and took their chances.

C-47A No. 43-15211, which would do the bulk of its World War Two military service with the 439th Troop Carrier Group, United States Army Air Forces, was completed and rolled out at the Long Beach, California factory of Douglas Aircraft on February 14th 1944 and delivered to the Air Force on the 19th. It was one of 2,954 C-47A-80-DLs produced in the Long Beach facility between 1941 and 1946.

This aeroplane was accepted as a part of the USAAF inventory on March 1st 1944 after only two hours and fifty-five minutes of test-flying. Its first military flight was to Mobile, Alabama, where it was fitted with long-range fuel ferry tanks and other military equipment prior to departing for Baer Field, Fort Wayne, Indiana, and the 1st Troop Carrier Processing Unit. There, it was assigned its first crew: 2nd Lieutenant Russell W. Barron-pilot, 2nd Lieutenant Charles A. Trimble-co-pilot, Corporal Jack H. Hadsell-crew chief, and Corporal Carmine P. Percaro-radio operator.

Army Special Orders Number 70 detailed the deployment of 43-15211, together with twenty-three other C-47As, many of them sister ships of '211 as part of the same construction batch. They were sent to Morrison Field, West Palm Beach, Florida, where the crew would receive secret orders regarding their final destination. These orders were not to be opened until the crew was two hours into the flight from West Palm Beach.

On March 15th the aircraft arrived at Morrison Field after a three and a half hour flight. They left the next day on a six-hour flight to Borinquen Field, Puerto Rico, and learned on opening their sealed orders that they were bound for the European Theatre of Operations. Their next stop, on March 17th, was Atkinson Field, Georgetown, British Guiana, a seven-hour trip, followed by a seven-hour leg to Belem, Brazil, flying over the Amazon delta and skirting "head-hunter" territory. Their final landfall on the South American continent was Natal, on the Atlantic coast of Brazil, after six and a half hours in the air.

The next stop for the crew would be Wideawake Field on tiny, volcanic Ascension Island in the mid-Atlantic. In poor weather conditions the thirty-five square mile speck might easily have been missed, but, thanks to the addition of radio compasses and beacons, the crew's eight-hour flight and the treacherous final approach through low cloud and severe turbulence was rewarded with a safe and welcome arrival.

After a few days rest on Ascension, the C-47 crew departed for Roberts Field, near Monrovia in Liberia, West Africa, a six and a quarter hour jaunt, followed by a five-hour leg to Dakar in French West Africa, where they arrived on March 25th, tired but in good spirits. The next stretch—eight and a half hours—was almost entirely over desert; their destination, Marrakech, Morocco, where they briefly visited the French part of town.

Putting Morocco behind them, the crew began the most dangerous part of the journey—a long flight to England across the Bay of Biscay, which was heavily patrolled by Junkers Ju 88s

and Messerschmitt Bf 110s of the German Air Force. A USAAF B-24 bomber had been shot down in the area the day before. But luck was with the '211 crew and they landed safely at RAF Valley, Anglesey, Wales, as ordered.

Following another brief rest period, they took the C-47 on to USAAF Station 462, Balderton, near Newark in Lincolnshire and parted company with the aeroplane that had brought them from America to Britain and to war. The crew and the aircraft would be assigned to the 92nd Troop Carrier Squadron of the 439th Troop Carrier Group, one of four squadrons making up that group, each with a full complement of eighteen C-47s.

The 439th was under the command of Major Charles H. Young, a former "barnstormer" pilot in the mid-1930s. Major Young, a native of Argonia, Kansas, entered Army pilot training as a cadet at Randolph Field, San Antonio, Texas, in October 1936. He was the first in his class to solo and his fifty-five-minute record still stands in the U.S. Air Force for minimum flight time with an instructor prior to soloing. On graduating, he served two years on active duty before joining American Airlines as a pilot flying the Douglas DC-3 Sleeper Transports. He was recalled to the Army in the spring of 1942 and helped in the organization of the Troop Carrier Command. In January 1944, he was appointed commander of the 439th, one of the youngest group commanders in the ETO. After the war he returned to American Airlines to complete a thirty-five-year career, ending as a Boeing 747 captain with nearly 27,500 flying hours in his logbooks.

2nd Lieutenant Lavern H. Mays, a native of Los Angeles, was assigned to the Troop Carrier Command in February 1943. He was sent to the 60th Troop Carrier Squadron, 63rd Troop Carrier Group, and in just two weeks, was checked out as a Pilot in Command and instructor for new co-pilots. His group was assigned to Fort Benning, Georgia, for training in dropping paratroopers, and then to Fort Bragg, North Carolina, where he and his fellow C-47 pilots flew jumps and glider towing exercises under combat conditions with the 101st Airborne Division. The 63rd became an overseas training group and Mays was promoted to 1st Lieutenant and Flight Leader/Instructor. He volunteered for overseas duty, arriving in England on May 30th 1944, where he was ordered to the 92nd Troop Carrier Squadron.

As a 1st Lieutenant with more than 800 hours flying C-47s, Verne Mays took part in some of the most significant and mem-

ON THE DC-3 PRODUCTION LINE AT SANTA MONICA IN 1939. BY THEN THE SANTA MONICA DOUGLAS FACTORY WAS STRUGGLING WITH THE PRODUCTION DEMANDS OF COMMERCIAL, MILITARY AND LEND-LEASE AIRCRAFT. BOTH THE FACTORY AND THE AIRFIELD ON WHICH IT WAS LOCATED WERE FAR TOO SMALL FOR THE COMPANY'S NEEDS AND MAJOR EXPANSION BEGAN WITH NEW CONSTRUCTION FACILITIES IN EL SEGUNDO NEAR THE PRESENT SITE OF THE LOS ANGELES AIRPORT, IN LONG BEACH AND IN OKLAHOMA CITY, OKLAHOMA.

orable airborne operations of the war, including Operation Dragoon, the Allied invasion of southern France, on August 15th 1944, only a few months after the D-Day landings at Normandy in northern France. One of the two aircraft he flew on the 15th was that same C-47A, 43-15211, now squadron-coded J8-B— the same aeroplane that half a century later would be owned and operated by shipping executive, Peter Livanos.

The 439th was based in a wheatfield outside of Orbetello, Italy

in August and Mays was assigned to fly J8-B in the glider-towing mission of that afternoon. It was the aeroplane normally flown by Major Cecil E. Petty, who would become commanding officer of the 92nd squadron. Vern had flown a four-hour para-drop mission that morning in another aircraft with Colonel Harry Tower, the 439th Executive Officer. As one of the most experienced C-47 pilots in the group, Mays was asked by Tower to fly with him as they led the forty-five-ship para-drop formation.

AN ACE IN THE HOLE

Ammunition almost gone . . . smoke streaking back from a shot-up engine . . . enemy fighters poised for a knockout blow. But helpless? No! This bomber pilot has an ace in the hole. As long as his radio keeps him in touch with the ground and supporting planes, he has what it takes to talk his way out of trouble. And this he can depend on! His Belmont-made equipment has had the blessing of accuracy by every hand that touched it.

Belmont employees are giving him the best that human hands can produce. And they are turning it out in great volume—on time! Some day, these same skilled hands again will be fashioning peacetime radios for you. And just as today we pledge our fighting men our best, so too, we pledge that Belmont's peacetime products will stand un-excelled—in engineering, in design and in performance. Belmont Radio Corp., Chicago.

Belmont Radio
TELEVISION • ELECTRONICS

Despite war restrictions, America's living standard is still the world's best —— thanks to U.S. industrial progress.

From Alice...to Eddie...to Adolf!

The drill whirs in Alice's hands . . . shaping a swift new plane . . . for Eddie to fly.

In Alice's mind is the memory of Eddie looking handsome as he left to join his squadron . . . the sweet sound of his words as he talked of the home they would some day have together.

They'd have it now if it weren't for Adolf. Alice and Eddie know why they're fighting.

Such are the human stories that lie behind the overwhelming production of planes, ships, tanks and guns that America is now pouring forth to beat the Axis.

In our fighting industries, millions of loyal Americans have turned their peacetime skills into wartime production. Texaco resources are already producing vast quantities of vitally important 100-octane aviation gasoline . . . chemicals for war explosives . . . high quality lubricating oils for the Navy, Army and Air Corps . . . and a host of other products.

To win, we all willingly drive our cars slower to save gasoline and tires, buy war bonds and stamps, conserve our food, clothing, metal.

For this is every American's war . . . Alice's, Eddie's, yours, ours. On one point we are all resolved: *it won't be Adolf's.*

THE TEXAS COMPANY
TEXACO FIRE-CHIEF AND SKY CHIEF GASOLINES
HAVOLINE AND TEXACO MOTOR OILS

The weather had been hot and dry with no recent rain and the airstrip was dusty. Water trucks had been sprinkling the surface all day on the 14th to keep the dust down. The take-off for the para-drop mission was set for midnight. It was led by Colonel Charles H. Young, commanding officer of the 439th, and the first take-offs were uneventful. However, as they continued, more and more dust was stirred up, reducing visibility for the pilots waiting their turn on the runway. When it was the turn of 1st Lieutenant Michael Drozda, piloting C-47 42-92735, the dust cloud churned up by the preceding aircraft was huge. Not only did it dramatically reduce his visibility, but the dust ingested by his engines before and during his take-off roll resulted in a critical loss of power, causing his plane to stall out at the point of leaving the ground. The C-47 veered to the right and careered off the strip directly towards the makeshift control tower, scattering the Group Operations Officer and others

there. The plane ground to a halt short of the tower and burst into flames. Many years later Mike Drozda stated that he believed that there had been no serious injuries to his crew or to any of the paratroopers on board. He, however, spent three months in an English hospital before being evacuated to Georgia where he had surgery on his right shoulder. He was in hospital for nearly eleven months before emerging with only limited use of his right arm.

Colonel Young, in the lead ship of the formation, passed his checkpoint on the northern tip of the island of Corsica and was flying his C-47 on autopilot and adhering strictly to his course. Ten minutes before their estimated landfall in southern France his navigator gave him a course correction of 15 degrees to the right, which surprised him as he was certain that the aircraft could not have strayed from their heading. Even so, Young became convinced that the navigator was correct. Young made the course correction and moments later was told by the navigator that they were crossing over the French coastline. Breaks in the heavy cloud cover then revealed a few lights, confirming their landfall. Continuing on course towards the drop zone, they arrived at a point four minutes from the drop and Young flipped the switch illuminating the "stand up and hook up" red light. He then slowed the aircraft to the required jumping airspeed and, as they neared the estimated drop point, hit the

switch for the green "drop" light and the paratroopers jumped into the night through the cloud layer with no assistance from their pathfinders.

Colonel Young believed he had delivered the airborne troops to their drop zone. He learned later from one of them, 3rd Battalion Commander Melvin Zais, that he had not. Zais told Young that his men had landed twelve miles from their assigned position and had cursed Colonel Young every step of the way as they force-marched back to the DZ. But when they finally arrived and saw the acres of sharpened stakes and poles sticking up from the drop zone, they were grateful to have missed it and glad to have walked the twelve miles. "We will be happy to jump with you again any time," Zais told Young. That was the only time the colonel missed a drop or landing zone during the entire war.

That same afternoon the dust was again a factor. It delayed the assembly of the towships and gliders. When Lt. Mays returned from the morning para-drop mission and was ordered to fly the afternoon glider mission in J8-B, he learned that he was to lead the 92nd Squadron as well. The forty-seven C-47s and CG-4A gliders made the trip in perfect formation and a bright, blue sky. When the mass of aircraft reached the French coast, the morning cloud and fog layer had lifted and most of the gliders were able to make reasonably safe landings. Colonel

ground fifteen to forty feet apart with taut wires stretched between them. Fortunately, the paratroopers had already cut the wires, making it possible for the glider pilots to weave their way between the obstacles and the majority landed safely. Even so, many of the gliders had their wings sheered off by the poles. Of the flight that August afternoon, Vern Mays recalled: "By the time we reached the French coast the fog had lifted and our gliders were able to land okay. Major Petty's crew chief had kept his plane in perfect condition and it performed beautifully for us."

Before Dragoon there was Overlord—the Allied invasion landings at Normandy on the Channel coast of France in June 1944. British military historian, lecturer and journalist, John Keegan: "As spring became summer in 1944, yet more exciting manifestations of American military power thrust themselves on our attention. The GIs whom we had got to know had, we now grasped, been engineers, builders and truck drivers, who had been creating settlements for the fighting troops still to come.

"They were now among us. And with them they brought a new wave of equipment, half-track scout cars, amphibious trucks and gigantic transporters, laden with tanks and bulldozers—a machine previously unknown in Britain—which held to the main roads and, when in convoy, were usually seen heading southward towards the ports of Hampshire and Dorset, on the Channel coast opposite France.

"American aircraft, too, appeared in great numbers, Liberators, Dakotas and occasionally the dramatically twin-boomed P-38 Lightning, glimpsed rocketing across the sky like a shape of things to come.

"Dakotas [C-47s] were the most common, and the source of the most arresting experience I underwent that fresh, green spring. Some forgotten journey brought me unexpectedly upon an airfield, over which a cloud of aircraft hung, turning and swooping. But it was unlike any formation I had ever seen, in that the planes were linked together in pairs by spider-thin cables. Suddenly and successively the cables fell slack and the second in each pair of aircraft began to descend towards the runway. Strangest of all, they had neither propellers nor engines, their descent was silent and, when they touched the ground, they came to a halt within a few yards. From their interiors men tumbled out and formed ranks, from which brilliant red and green flares were shot in sputtering arcs towards the departing

Young wrote later, however, that they had encountered some congestion over the two LZs, with many of the aircraft and a number of supporting P-51 fighters seeming to go in all directions at once, and visibility on the approach to the LZ hampered by smoke from battle in two of the nearby harbours. After passing Corsica on the way to France, one of the gliders had to be ditched in the sea when it developed a structural weakness. The personnel aboard were later rescued. All of the C-47s and nearly all of the gliders reached the landing zones. The congestion described by Colonel Young happened when several aircraft from the various participating groups arrived later than their assigned times over the landing zones, creating chaos and dangerous delays.

In the congestion, most of the gliders were released at higher than intended altitudes, but somehow the glider pilots managed to manoeuvre and dodge one another in their landing approaches. As they came down, they were shocked to see that the landing zones were studded with obstacles—poles set in the

Dakota tugs. I had had my first sight of a method of war which I had not dreamt, a glider assault on the rear of the enemy.

"But not my last. One evening some weeks later [on the night of June 5th 1944] the sky over our house began to fill with the sound of aircraft, which swelled until it overflowed the darkness from edge to edge. Its first tremors had taken my parents into the garden, and as the roar grew I followed and stood between them to gaze awestruck at the constellation of red, green and yellow lights which rode across the heavens and streamed southward towards the sea. It seemed as if every aircraft in the world was in flight, as wave followed wave without intermission, dimly discernible as darker corpuscles on the black plasma of the clouds, which the moon had not yet risen to illuminate. The element of noise in which they swam became solid, blocking our ears, entering our lungs and beating the ground beneath our feet with the relentless surge of an ocean swell. Long after the last had passed from view and the thunder of their passage had died into the silence of the night, restoring to our con-

N1944A AT KIDLINGTON AIRPORT; RIGHT: VISITING GOODWOOD; BELOW RIGHT: PASSING THE ISLE OF WIGHT; FAR RIGHT: PILOT ANDREW DAVENPORT AND COPILOT JOHN TODD IN THE COCKPIT OF N1944A.

sciousness the familiar and timeless elements of our surroundings, elms, hedges, rooftops, clouds and stars, we remained transfixed and wordless on the spot where we stood, gripped by a wild surmise at what the power, majesty and menace of the great migratory flight could portend.

"Next day we knew. The Americans had gone. The camps they had built had emptied overnight. The roads were deserted. No doubt, had we been keeping check, we would have noticed a gradual efflux of their numbers. But it had been disguised until the last moment and the outrush had then been sudden. The BBC news bulletin told us why. 'Early this morning units of the Allied armies began landing on the coast of France.' "

In the very early hours of June 6th 1944, Major Cecil Petty, flying 43-15211, the C-47 coded J8-B, from its base at Upottery in Devon, England, dropped elements of the 1st Battalion, 506th Parachute Infantry Regiment near Drop Zone "C" in Normandy. The DZ was situated close by Sainte Marie du-Mont, but most of the paratroopers landed near the village of Ecoquenauville,

between the DZ and the town of Sainte-Mère Eglise.

The 506th PIR had been activated in July 1942 at Mount Currahee, Camp Toccoa, Georgia, as part of the new 101st Airborne Division. The regiment took its motto from the Cherokee Indian word, Currahee, meaning "Stands Alone." In September of 1943 it deployed to England where it continued training for the Normandy invasion. When the men of the 506th jumped into the black sky of northern France that June night, they were tasked with the seizure of the high ground directly behind the landing beaches.

They had left England at 1:00 a.m. on the 6th. As they crossed the French coast, a thick low-cloud layer coupled with intense

LEFT: AFTER ACQUISITION BY WINGS VENTURE IN 1997, N1944A WAS FLOWN TO ENGLAND AND RESTORED TO ITS ORIGINAL PARATROOP-CARRYING CONFIGURATION. THE WORK WAS DONE BY PERSONAL PLANE SERVICES AT WYCOMBE AIR PARK NEAR MARLOW, BUCKS; FAR LEFT: FRANCO TAMBASCIA REFUELLING THE C-47 AT KIDLINGTON AIRPORT.

DZ. These two planeloads of paratroopers quickly reorganized themselves and succeeded in capturing their objectives—two bridges over the Douvre River. The men of the 506th battalion, though scattered, managed to join up into small fighting groups and, before the arrival of the initial seaborne landing forces on the invasion beaches, were able to capture nearly all their objectives and secure most of the high ground overlooking those beaches. They included the men of Easy Company—some of whose extraordinary exploits are described in the chapter, AT WAR, and in the book *Band of Brothers* by Stephen E. Ambrose, and featured in the television series of the same title. General Maxwell Taylor, commander of the 101st Airborne Division, had promised his troops they would be relieved and returned to England after three days of battle in Normandy. They were involved in the fight in Carentan for thirty-three days.

U.S. Army General John R. Galvin, who from June 1987 to June 1992 served as Supreme Allied Commander, Europe and Commander-in-Chief, United States European Command, wrote of the D-Day operation: ". . . all three airborne divisions [the 101st, 82nd, and the British 6 Airborne] were able to report that their major missions had been accomplished. The British 6th held the crossings over the Orne south of Caen; the 82nd controlled Sainte-Mère Eglise and the crossings over the Merderet; the 101st had opened the four exits off the beach and dominated the crossings over the Douvre. Although the paratroopers fought through their first hours in Normandy as semi-isolated battalion fragments, all three airborne divisions were able to take over operational control by the end of the day and coordinate the continuing push to expand the beachhead."

Allied casualties of June 6th are estimated at approximately 6,600 Americans killed, missing or wounded, including 2,500 airborne personnel. British casualties are estimated at 2,750 killed, missing or wounded, including 650 from 6 Airborne. Canadian casualties are estimated at 946. German casualties for that day are estimated at between 4,000 and 9,000. Out of approximately 2,000 men from the 506th who jumped into France that night, 231 were killed, 183 were missing or prisoners of war, and 569 were wounded—a casualty rate of roughly 50 percent. For their achievements on D-Day and in the following month, the regiment was awarded the Presidential Unit Citation.

enemy flak scattered the eighty-one C-47s of the airborne force so widely that only nine of the planes managed to deliver their paratroopers precisely over the drop zone. Their particular role in the activities of D-Day was code-named Operation Chicago. Their erratic jump patterns, due to the heavy flak, caused many of them to land as much as twenty miles from their designated landing positions. As it happened, the Germans were ready and waiting for those men who did arrive on their assigned drop zone. Within the first ten minutes of the drop, enemy troops had killed the American battalion commander, his executive officer, and much of the 3rd Battalion. The only members of that battalion to survive were those who came down outside of their

After D-Day, the 439th Troop Carrier Group, and C-47 J8-B,

flew a mission from Upottery on June 7th. They brought additional troops into Normandy in a combination of fifty Horsa and Waco gliders which were released over Landing Zone "W" about three miles south of Sainte-Mère Eglise. The trip was uneventful except for one C-47 with engine trouble which landed safely at Warmwell, near Poole in Dorset. Over the next few weeks, while new landing strips were being prepared in northern France for the Allies and supply lines were being arranged, there was very little for the flight crews and airborne troops to do. It fell to the squadron commanders to channel the energies of the men in the interim. Their solutions ranged from the frivolous to the educationally worthwhile and included staged aerobatics, wing-walking and other stunts, ground contests such as pari-mutuel bicycle races, tug-of-war, greased-pig-catching, and glider spot-landing competitions between the four squadrons. There were also demonstrations of how a C-47 could lift three gliders at once and how it might be made to evade an attacking enemy fighter plane. Obviously, the C-47 could not outrun the fighter, but the microphone and ear-phone-equipped crew chief in the astrodome could inform the pilot of the fighter's location and distance from the transport. As the enemy plane got close enough to open fire, the C-47 pilot would slow his aircraft, lower his landing gear and flaps, throw the big plane into a hard 90-degree left or right turn and drop it behind one of southern England's many low hills. Such evasions frequently worked, at least in exercises, as the fighter, with its relatively heavier wing-loading, could not stay with the C-47 in the manoeuvre.

On June 24th, J8-B and seventy-four other C-47s of the 439th flew a vital resupply mission out of the Greenham Common and Ramsbury air bases in southern England into the A-2 and A-6 airfields behind the Utah beachhead in Normandy. The transport aircraft were escorted by Spitfires and P-47 Thunderbolt fighters. It is believed that the cargoes of the C-47s that day were mainly ammunition—probably a mixture of 105mm and 155mm shells, and .30 calibre rounds for use in the continuing fighting on the Cotentin Peninsula. The transports returned to Upottery in a medical evacuation mission, repatriating Allied wounded from the invasion battle.

When the Allies launched Operation Market-Garden, it was the largest corps-sized airborne drop in history. Riding high on the success of the Normandy and southern France invasions, Allied planners devised an intriguing but unrealistically aggressive scheme for invading German-occupied Holland. In it, British Field Marshal Bernard Montgomery was to head the Allied armies across the lower Rhine River at Arnhem. It was a two-part operation. The ground assault part was code-named Garden; the objectives of the three simultaneous, coordinated daylight airborne troop-carrier operations, called Market, were German targets in Arnhem, Nijmegen and Eindhoven. The drop zones were as much as eighty-five miles into enemy territory. The job of the airborne forces was to open a sixty-mile-long corridor for the ground forces, and the airborne assault aspect was planned to take three days, beginning on September 17th.

On that day the 439th, and J8-B, were flying from Balderton airfield in Nottinghamshire. The group was to drop 388 paratroopers to the south of Nijmegen. They flew in multiple lanes along two separate air routes in order to reduce the time over the DZ for the group. Their accuracy over the course of the operation was excellent, even though they experienced a weather delay on the second day.

The Allies had overstretched their supply lines into Europe after the landings in Normandy and southern France and the advance of many units was halted by their lack of gasoline, food and ammunition. When not required to fly airborne missions, some of the troop carrier aircraft were used to bring these supplies to the front, weather permitting.

The enemy resistance in Holland was surprisingly heavy, but the Americans managed to take their objectives when aided by advancing British ground and armoured elements. The British plan, however, could not succeed. Commanders ignored or discounted intelligence information and photographs provided by the Dutch underground, which proved that two German panzer divisions were refitting in the Arnhem area and posing a massive and powerful threat to the Allies. In another critical error, the drop zone established for the Arnhem sector was located much too far from the Rhine bridge—the primary British objective in the sector. And, in a further example of wishful thinking, the plan required three consecutive days of good weather over the North Sea for the airborne operation, when it was well known that the weather there in September was unpredictable. One of the most critical failures of the overall operation was poor Allied communications in Holland. So poor were they, that

operational control was often totally jeopardized. Furthermore, there was no ground-to-air communication, which caused a two-day delay in the arrival of reinforcements to the Arnhem sector.

The lives of many C-47 airmen were lost in the effort to bring the desperately-needed troop reinforcements and supplies to the areas—some of which had already been lost to the enemy.

While stationed at A-39, Chateaudun, between the French towns of Orleans and Le Mans, the 439th was called on to fly troop-transport, supply-drop, and medical evacuation missions in support of the counter-offensive against German forces in the Ardennes—the Battle of the Bulge. The German offensive had begun December 16th and caused the Allied troop carrier units to begin airlifting some 11,000 men of the 17th Airborne Division from England to the Reims area in a series of night flights between December 22nd and 29th. During Operation Repulse, the 439th and other units of the IX Troop Carrier Command participated in an intensive routine of troop transport and resupply activity, including resupply of the 101st Airborne troops then struggling to hold out in the southeastern Belgian town of Bastogne, besieged by German forces. Of the 2,127 sorties flown in that period by the C-47s, 927 were flown to Bastogne. The deliveries included gasoline, food, fifty gliders carrying heavy ammunition and a team of army surgeons.

With ammunition for the artillery at a critically low ebb by Christmas Day, two 50th Troop Carrier Wing groups based in France, the 439th and 440th, received an urgent request that a special glider mission be flown in on the 26th. Weather conditions in England prevented any such missions originating there, so it was up to those two groups in France to carry the freight. The mission was then delayed until the 27th.

Bringing in seventy-six tons of 155mm artillery shells was challenge enough in reasonable circumstances, but on this occasion the situation was made worse when insufficient numbers of the scheduled protecting fighters showed up to do their job. Enemy flak was intense and concentrated and 26 percent of the C-47s were shot down. Only the courage and determination of the air crews and glider pilots made possible the safe delivery of more than 70 percent of the cargo to the landing zones.

The pilot of 049, one of the glider-towing C-47s, was Joe Fry, his co-pilot, George Weisfeld. The flight was mostly uneventful until the group was approaching the Bastogne area. Nearing the landing zone, 049 was hit by flak in the belly of the aircraft, aft of the wing trailing edge. A fuel tank must have been ruptured as a fire suddenly broke out and began to take hold in the main cabin. Fry ordered his crew to bail out and the radio operator and crew chief left immediately. Co-pilot Weisfeld, though, chose to help Fry control the aeroplane to the glider release point and said: "Joe, I'll stay with you until you're ready to leave."

As they neared the release point, flames from the C-47 had reached half way along the tow-rope to the glider being flown by J.D. Hill. Hill released his glider from the rope and Joe Fry told Weisfeld: "Let's get out of this son of a bitch before it blows up." The co-pilot made it through the cabin and jumped from the back hatch, but was severely burned in the process. Fry, meanwhile, did his best to stabilize the aircraft and set the autopilot. He put on his chest parachute pack and opened the cabin door. The entire cabin was then afire and impassable. Closing the door, he re-entered the cockpit and jettisoned the top escape hatch. Climbing out into the windstream, he was surprised by the minimal wind blast and realized that the plane must be close to stalling out. He began crawling back along the top of the fuselage, hoping that he wouldn't slip and fall into one of the propellers. As he passed the astrodome he looked down and saw that the fire was then consuming the crew compartment. His memory of the experience briefly blanks out at that point. His next recollection is of dangling behind the shroud lines of his parachute, above and behind the tail section of the C-47. Evidently, he had either jumped or been thrown off the left side of the burning aeroplane and had hit the left horizontal stabilizer, his 'chute wrapping around the leading edge when the pack split open, allowing the parachute to stream out. Ground witnesses to the incident stated that the plane was no more than 300 feet up at that moment. No one is certain about what happened next. Fry thought that the aeroplane either exploded or melted apart at that point. The drag of the 'chute and Fry's weight pulled him free of the stabilizer and the parachute then inflated just enough to deposit him safely in the snow. He had bruises and burns and an injured right leg, and his uniform was saturated with melted aluminium, but he had survived, landing just inside Allied lines. Some 101st Airborne troops nearby ran over and dragged Fry to their rifle pit where they plied him with cognac.

Upottery, USAAF Station 462, was located in Devon in the southwest of England, between Exeter and Taunton. Originally built for American medium bombers, Upottery was first occupied by the C-47s of the 439th TCG on April 26th 1944, when the group moved from its training base in England at Balderton. Constructed with three runways, two hangars and many aircraft dispersals, it was also furnished with a variety of Nissen huts and other typical air base buildings of the time—all of which served the needs of the 439th until the bulk of the organization departed for a new assignment in Orbetello, Italy, on July 17th. The air echelon returned to operate from Upottery on a few occasions before taking up other temporary residences at new airfields in France during September. Upottery airfield was then occupied by PB4Y-1 units of the U.S. Navy, flying anti-submarine patrols for the duration of the war. The air base was closed in November 1948. Much physical evidence of its existence remains in 2008, as illustrated by the accompanying images, some of which were photographed from the C-47 J8-B.

Training for Operation Varsity, the Allies' crossing of the Rhine River into Germany, took place during January and February 1945. Some 50,000 flying hours were logged, of which 21,000 were formation practice and 9,000 were glider towing. The balance related to instrument flying, navigation and transition flying for replacement personnel. Just under 20,000 paratrooper jumps were made. With the relocation of the 50th Wing to France the preceding fall, its groups practised a total of 4,329 glider tows during the first half of March. In the run-up to Varsity, most of the Wing C-47s had been re-equipped with self-sealing fuel tanks. Reinforced noses and parachute arresters had been added to the gliders. Improvements were made to navigational methods. The glider pilots, in addition to having increased infantry training, were required to make a minimum of five practice landings a month. Combat Control Teams were organized to improve communication links with ground troops and the air resupply missions, as well as the coordination of battlefield medical evacuation—a procedure pioneered by members of the 439th Group in the Remagen area on the Rhine. Additionally, Allied night and day fighters were provided by the U.S. Ninth Air Force beginning March 20th, to protect the bases used by the troop carrier groups in France.

Operation Varsity was to be the largest one-day airborne assault

ABOVE: AIR TROOPS OF THE NINTH U.S. ARMY INFANTRY, FORT SAM HOUSTON, TEXAS, PRACTISE LOADING AND UNLOADING ANTI-TANK EQUIPMENT IN AN ARMY TRANSPORT AIRCRAFT AT DUNCAN FIELD IN JULY 1941; LEFT: U.S. ARMY PRACTISE JUMPS EARLY IN THE WAR.

LEFT: THE CRUMBLING CONTROL TOWER AT THE DEVON, ENGLAND BASE, UPOTTERY, FROM WHICH N1944A AND EIGHTY OTHER C-47S TOOK OFF IN THEIR PARA-DROP AND GLIDER MISSIONS OF D-DAY, JUNE 6TH 1944; BELOW: PART OF A LOCAL RECEPTION FOR TWO 'EASY COMPANY' U.S. ARMY VETERANS, DON MALARKEY AND EARL MCCLUNG, REVISITING THEIR FORMER BASE IN 2008 FOR THE FIRST TIME SINCE 1944. THE C-47 N1944A WAS FLOWN TO UPOTTERY TO HONOUR THE FORMER 'BAND OF BROTHERS' SOLDIERS.

mission of all time. Those doing the planning felt they had learned a thing or two from the mistakes of Arnhem. This time the airborne operation would be completed in daylight, moving more than 17,000 airborne troops, 7,000,000 pounds of supplies and equipment, 1,200 vehicles, 130 artillery guns, to a relatively small DZ/LZ area behind enemy lines. They would do the job with 1,836 transport aircraft and 1,348 gliders. The whole plan hinged on being able to contain the enormous enemy resistance anticipated when the Allied forces entered Germany. It depended heavily on Allied capture of the bridges across the Issel River and on quick crossings enabling the Allied forces to negotiate the flood plain rapidly and reach the Ruhr industrial area.

To expedite the airborne effort, the air formations would employ three lanes and one additional lane at a higher altitude. There was also to be an assembly of 240 B-24 Liberator bombers bringing further supplies to be dropped fifteen minutes after the troop carrier formation. So great was this combined air fleet that more than three hours were required for it to pass a given point on its route to the Rhine.

With few exceptions, the troop carrier deliveries arrived with amazing accuracy, but the operation was not without problems. The nearby German town of Wesel was burning furiously—the result of an earlier Allied shelling—as the transport aircraft came into the area. The fires created immense smoke plumes, shrouding the drop and landing zones in smoke more than 2,000 feet thick in places. The troop carriers were further threatened by having to fly through the heaviest concentration of anti-aircraft fire yet experienced in an airborne operation. In the action, 394 IX Troop Carrier Command aircraft were hit by the flak and more than half of the gliders descending into Landing Zone S were hit on the way down.

In spite of the intense air and ground opposition put up by the Germans in the drop and landing zone areas, the airborne operation and the Rhine crossing were successful, causing Supreme Allied Commander General Dwight Eisenhower to say of the operation: "It sealed the fate of Germany."

In March 1945, Vern Mays was promoted to the rank of captain and between April 8th and 22nd he flew eight additional 439th TCG C-47 resupply missions, carrying food, clothing, medicine, gasoline, ordnance equipment and other supplies to the front

lines and evacuating patients to rear zone hospitals. In these last eight wartime missions, he logged 58.10 flying hours.

The highest ranking airborne commander of the war, General Mathew Ridgeway, referred to the troop carrier pilots: ". . . as skilled as any aviators I ever knew, and God knows they were brave men, both in the air and on the ground. In the run to the drop zone, they flew formations tighter and more precise than any the bombers ever flew, and they did it at night. They couldn't take evasive action, either, no matter how hot the fire from the ground might be."

One of the last military assignments given to the C-47s of the 439th TCG was the repatriation of Allied prisoners of war from camps in Germany to France. The C-47 J8-B served in that capacity during May 1945. After the war, it served with several air force units in Germany and is believed to have participated in the Berlin Airlift.

In November 1950, J8-B was transferred to the government of Norway as part of the Mutual Defense Aid Program, and later to the Danish Air Force under the same program, where it was modified with the installation of pollution-measuring equipment and operated by the Danish Atomic Commission. In August 1976 the aeroplane was leased to Twickenham Film Studios for use in the movie *A Bridge Too Far*, for which it was painted to represent the USAAF C-47 337185, "CF-3", as well as the RAF Dakota KG912, in the Arnhem operation. Declared surplus to inventory by Denmark in September 1982, the plane was acquired by Valiant Air Command of Titusville, Florida, in the fall of 1983. It was purchased in September 1988 by Doan Helicopter, a Florida company, for restoration. At that time the airframe had logged 15,833 flying hours. The next owner was Wings Venture, of Connecticut, which ferried the C-47 to the UK in 1999 to undergo a major interior refit in which it was reconfigured to an original troop carrier layout.

Peter Livanos has owned and operated N1944A for eleven years. The C-47 takes pride of place in his growing collection of military aircraft with particularly compelling histories. In addition to its participation in D-Day and the invasion of southern France, as well as Arnhem, it is believed that N1944A took part in the Berlin Airlift while based in Germany during 1948-49.

TOP LEFT: THE GLIDER TOW CABLE HOOK-UP TO A C-47; ABOVE: A MASS FORMATION OF C-47S HEADING FOR HOLLAND IN THE ARNHEM OPERATION, MARKET GARDEN, OF SEPTEMBER 1944; TOP RIGHT: PARATROOPERS EN ROUTE TO JUMP IN THE INVASION OF SOUTHERN FRANCE, OPERATION DRAGOON, AUGUST 15TH 1944; LEFT: A C-47 TAKES OFF WITH A HORSA GLIDER IN TOW HEADING FOR NORMANDY FROM AN ENGLISH AIRFIELD ON D-DAY, JUNE 6TH 1944; RIGHT: U.S. ARMY PARATROOPERS ARE DROPPED AT LOW LEVEL BY C-47S OVER NORTHERN FRANCE ON D-DAY.

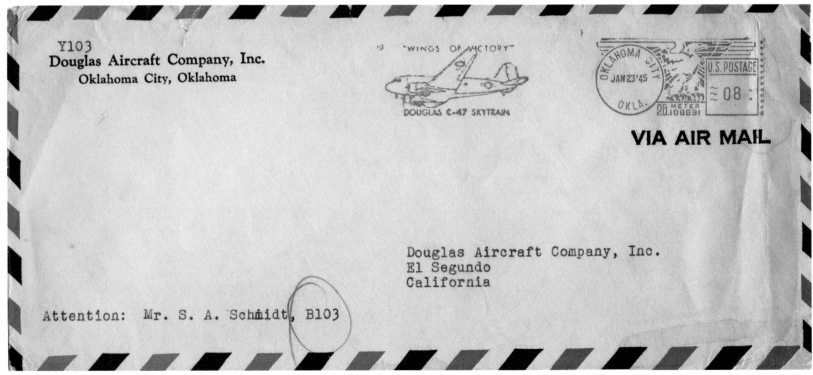

VETERANS OF EASY COMPANY, 506TH PARACHUTE INFANTRY REGIMENT, 101ST AIRBORNE DIVISION, U.S.ARMY, EARL MCCLUNG, FAR LEFT, AND DON MALARKEY, LEFT, ARE SHOWN IN JULY 2008 REVISITING UPOTTERY, THE AIRFIELD IN DEVON, ENGLAND WHERE THEY DEPARTED BY C-47 AT AROUND MIDNIGHT OF JUNE 5TH 1944 FOR THEIR DROP BEHIND UTAH BEACH ON THE NORMANDY COAST AND THEIR PART IN THE D-DAY ASSAULT. THE MEN OF EASY COMPANY WERE COMMEMORATED IN THE BOOK AND TELEVISION SERIES *BAND OF BROTHERS*; TOP: C-47S EN ROUTE FROM BASES IN ENGLAND TO D-DAY DROP ZONES IN FRANCE; FAR LEFT ABOVE: A DOUGLAS C-53 SKYTROOPER NEAR WRIGHT FIELD, OHIO, IN THE 1940S.

THE AIRLINES

A.G. Leonard Morgan, one of the great aviators of all time, died March 11th 2005, age eighty-two. Len Morgan is remembered as a delightful columnist and author, and as a Braniff airline pilot of enormous experience. He flew every type of aircraft his company operated, from the DC-3 to the Boeing 747, as a captain in them all. He wrote more than thirty books on aviation subjects and hundreds of columns and articles for *Flying* magazine in the United States. Born in Indiana in 1923, Morgan volunteered for the Royal Canadian Air Force in 1941 and, following the Japanese attack on Pearl Harbor, transferred to the U.S. Army Air Forces where he flew C-47s in Egypt, Africa and the Middle East. Captain Morgan:"The C-47 groaned, it protested, it rattled, it leaked oil, it ran hot, it ran cold, it ran rough, it staggered along on hot days and scared you half to death. Its wings flexed and twisted in a horrifying manner, it sank back to earth with a great sigh of relief—but it flew and it flew and it flew. It took us and ten thousand crews around the globe to where we had to go and brought us home again, honest, faithful and magnificent machine that it was.

"The war ended and four frustrating years drifted past while I looked for airline employment. When, at long last, a job with a major trunk line opened up it was, happily, with an outfit operating a good number of DC-3s.

"Compared with military flying, the airline life was almost too good to be true. Fifteen minutes before departure you got aboard a nice clean airplane and took your place in a nice clean cockpit. The tanks were fuelled, the windshield wiped clean and the logbook carried no long lists of uncorrected gripes. The radios and other cockpit equipment were all in good working order. A truck outside pumped the ship full of refrigerated air. Half a dozen men bustled about underneath, doing all the chores left to a co-pilot in the Army. Twenty-one well-dressed civilians filled the seats and, promptly on schedule, you fired up and sped this happy load away to another splendid airfield equipped with concrete runways, adequate night lighting and navigational facilities that worked all of the time.

"The gross load was limited to 25,200 pounds, which was hardly half a load. During flight you had but to press a button

84

PRECEDING SPREAD: A JIG-
SAW PUZZLE OF THE 1940S;
ABOVE: AN AIRLINE DINNER
PLATE FROM A DC-3.

three times and a sweet young thing appeared in your working quarters with a round of really good, really hot coffee. On layovers you slept in air-conditioned hotels and, upon completion of the trip, you simply walked off the plane and went home. This was flying the way it was meant to be!

"Within a few months we junior fellows had grown accustomed to this white collar way of flying, accepted it as no more than our due and were grousing as loudly as the older heads about lousy schedules and the failure of the management to add new trips fast enough. But it was mostly talk for we all recognized our luck in being among the handful of ex-service airmen able to continue flying. It was, all in all, a most pleasant way to earn a living. It was, in fact, downright fun and most of us would have taken the job had it only paid off in meals and a place to sleep.

"When employed at the task for which it was originally designed, that of hauling passengers and mail in scheduled airline service, the DC-3 gave an excellent account of itself. It was a pleasure to ride and a pleasure to fly. It was the perfect training ship for pilots interested in airline careers, forgiving of mistakes, demanding enough to keep you on your toes. Almost every jet crew flying in the Free World today got its first heavy airplane experience in the DC-3.

"From the lower levels in which we worked the view of the earth beneath was generally excellent. This means something when you fly the same routes year after year and is one reason, I suspect, why pilots retain a favourable impression of their DC-3 days. At 5,000 feet you can see where you are going and appreciate the relationship of your machine to the terrain it covers. A favourite trip took us to Chicago with seven stops enroute. For eight hours the Midwest unrolled before us, slowly enough for sightseeing, rapidly enough to prevent boredom. We took off at dawn and climbed out across empty streets. Dropping down at Oklahoma City an hour later we saw the earliest risers back down from their driveways and scurry off to work. Yellow school buses began to speed along the red roads, pausing at farms while tiny dots got aboard. Wichita's streets were always jammed with cars, most heading toward the city. Topeka and Kansas City were relatively quiet when seen from above, with downtown parking lots filled to capacity and little traffic moving except near suburban shopping centres. Plodding northeastward in the midday hours we saw little change in the activity below. Men worked, continued on page 95

ABOVE: A 1948 AMERICAN AIRLINES GUIDE BOOK FOR PASSENGERS ON ITS DC-3 FLAGSHIPS; RIGHT: AN AMERICAN AIRLINES STEWARDESS IN THE 1950S.

DOUGLAS *Luxury* AIRLINERS
powered by
WRIGHT CYCLONE ENGINES

TWA

"The Lindbergh Line"
SHORTEST ROUTE
COAST TO COAST

PENNSYLVANIA
PCA
CENTRAL

SILA
SWEDISH INTERCONTINENTAL AIRLINES

RHODESIAN
and
NYASALAND
LIMITED
AIRWAYS

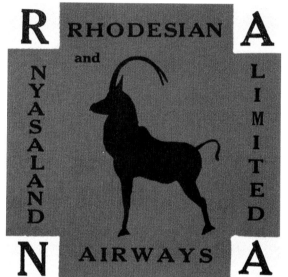

ROYAL DUTCH AIR LINES ★ HOLLAND

KLM

COAST TO COAST
CANADA TO THE GULF
AA
AMERICAN AIRWAYS Inc.

A SAMPLING OF AIRLINE
LUGGAGE LABELS MOSTLY
FROM THE ERA OF THE DC-3'S
COMMERCIAL SERVICE.

AIR DISPATCH

TO.................
ON
ARRIVAL
PHONE.................. or ....
ADDRESS..................
CITY..................
VIA BONANZA AIR LINES

U.S. AIR MAIL   AIR TRAVEL

EASTERN AIR TRANSPORT INC.

DETROIT · CLEVELAND · CHICAGO

VIA
U.S. MAIL
TAC
Transamerican
Airlines Corp.

ILLINOIS · INDIANA
MICHIGAN · OHIO

TOLEDO · SOUTH BEND · FT. WAYNE

JERSEY AIRWAYS LIMITED
JA

FLY TO THE
Convention
IT'S NEARER
by
Flagship
AMERICAN
AIRLINES
Inc.

KLM
KONI
The Flying Dutchman

BELOW: A THIMBLE PAINTED
TO COMMEMORATE THE DC-3.

DOUGLAS DC-3

A-B AEROTRANSPORT

A·B·A SWEDISH AIR LINES

PAGES 96-97:
THE NORTHWEST AIRLINES TICKET COUNTER AT FELTS FIELD, SPOKANE, WASHING-TON IN 1936. THE FLYING LOGBOOK OF TWA DC-3 PILOT FRANK D. BUEHL.

women shopped, children were in school, their buses waiting in neat rows behind their country classrooms. Farmers made geometric designs in the black soil or sped along dirt roads in pickup trucks leaving plumes of dust.

"We ate our lunch, a box of sandwiches with a small salad and Dixie cup of milk, threw the leftovers out of the window and rang for fresh coffee. As we lifted for the eighth time and laid the nose on Chicago, the school buses were already beginning to scatter to the farms, stopping now and then while tiny dots ran off. The turnpikes leading from the giant city ahead now carried their heaviest flow in the outbound lanes. Long commuter trains snaked westward, four miles apart.

"Flying VFR [visual flight rules] most of the time, we were free to drop down and check the progress on a new dam and guess at the shape of the lake it would form, watch the reapers swim across the golden land of Kansas, admire the skill of a Mississippi pilot edging his tow into a lock or simply enjoy the grandeur of the American Midwest. Farm lads looked up and envied us; we looked down and remembered. It was, as I say, a most pleasant way to earn a living.

"Most of the time, at least. There were times when you cursed the job and imagined yourself safe behind a desk in some solid ground work. On hot summer days you pitched along by the hour and made the passengers sick when a pressurized cabin would have put you on top of the turbulence and in cooler air. You bucked headwinds that reduced groundspeed to eighty miles an hour. You ran along the edges of line squalls at night, waiting for lightning flashes to illuminate cloud bases. You emerged from rain showers soaked to the skin for the cockpit leaked water like a sieve. You got caught in thunderstorms and fought to keep the airspeed within forty miles of a safe figure and the ship more or less right side up. You watched it fall from under you, even with the engines howling at climb power. You sweated out crosswinds on icy runways. You hated your seniors with their pressurization, radar, fancy navigation gear, tricycle wheels and reversing props. The DC-3 took second place to no other airplane in being able to give you a hairy ride.

"We tend to remember the pleasant and minimize the unpleasant in our memories of those activities we basically enjoy. So it is that I've almost forgotten the leaky windshield of a DC-3. Instead, I remember, and quite clearly, how nice it was to fly across the countryside in the early evening and watch the

| Date | AIRCRAFT FLOWN | | | CROSS COUNTRY | | REMARKS |
	Type	License Number	Type Engine	From	To	
9-24-46	DC-3			KC	LG	
9-25-46	DC-3			LG	PT	
9-25-46	DC-3			PT	KC	.
9-27-46	DC-3			KC	PT	
9-29-46	DC-3			PT	KC	
10-18-46	DC-3			KC	DT	
10-19-46	DC-3			DT	KC	
12-2-46	DC-3			KC	KC	TEST
12-5-46	DC-3			KC	LG	
12-6-46	DC-3			LG	KC	ISTRUMENT CHECK J. HENDRIX
12-11-46	DC-3			KC	NK	
12-12-46	DC-3			NK	KC	
12-16-46	DC-3			KC	NK	
12-17-46	DC-3			NK	LG	FERRY
12-17-46	DC-3			LG	KC	
12-20-46	DC-3			AB	KC	
12-21-46	DC-3			DRx	DRx	TEST
12-22-46	DC-3			DRx	KC	FERRY
12-22-46	DC-3			KC	CG	

CERTIFIED CORRECT	PILOT'S SIGNATURE	Page Total
	Frank D. Buehl	Brought Forward
		Total to Date

lighted towns drift slowly toward us and drop beneath the wings.

"Twenty-one was an ideal number of people to carry on an airplane. Cabin atmosphere in a DC-3 was informal, relaxed and conducive to friendly across-the-aisle chats. There was time to take in the view, and a view to take in. There was time to enjoy the meal, read your paper or be lulled into a nap by the hypnotic drone of the engines. The names of the crew appeared on the cockpit door, an indication of the more personalized nature of air travel then. After lunch an announcement form with the blank spaces pencilled in would be handed back along the seats. 'Welcome aboard Flight 24. We are cruising at 6,000 feet. Our groundspeed is 172 miles an hour. Our estimated time of arrival at St Louis is 2:47 p.m. Please tell your stewardess, Miss Adams, if there is anything we can do to make your trip more comfortable.' – Captain Bob Ford

"Up front the atmosphere was just as relaxed with collars loosened, feet propped up and little talk in the headsets. The countryside unrolled like a huge map, the familiar checkpoints taking shape and disappearing in slow but steady sequence.

"In comparison, the cabin of today's airliner resembles the

Aircraft Classification			Hood	Instrument	Trainer	Day	Night	Total Reg.	Total Co-Pilot
						217	402		619
						57	120		212
						537			537
						508	508		508
							507		507
							509		509
							358		358
							48		48
						616			616
						497	341		838
						428	217		645
			45			58	722		820
				100		232	407		639
							20		20
						229	614		843
						422			422
							7		7
							18		18
						210			210
			145			3703	5048		8751
			7355	5245	7330	142658	47839	119105	71432
			7358	5430	7330	146401	52927	119105	80243

SEMI-ANNUAL INSTRUMENT CHECK C.A.R. 61

CHECKED BY .... DATE 2-6-46

CERTIFIED BY .... E.S. Rickenbacker

Holland Tunnel with seats. Two, three or four harried girls work frantically to dish up food for a hundred people in fifty minutes. There is no time to meet the man across the aisle or have a second cup of coffee. The earth beneath looks like a dirty grey blanket. Your crew works behind a locked door now, their headsets filled with endless chatter between planes and ground controllers. Your pilots are concerned with a score of problems unknown twenty years ago. There is nothing relaxed about their work now. But this is the Air Age we yearned for and these are some of the changes it has brought. Who among us, passenger or pilot, would return to the ways of yesterday?"

The famed American World War One fighter ace Captain Eddie Rickenbacker (October 8th 1890-July 27th 1973) was a recipient of the Congressional Medal of Honor. Fascinated by most things mechanical, he was a largely self-taught engineer who worked in a Pennsylvania Railroad machine shop prior to becoming a racing driver, running in the Indianapolis 500 four times. His best and only finish was in the 1914 event in which continued on page 101

AN AIRLINE CAPTAIN CANDY
DISPENSER; LEFT: A DC-3
OF SILVER CITY AIRWAYS
BOARDING PASSENGERS IN
THE LIBYAN DESERT
DURING 1958.

TOP: A MOHAWK AIRLINES
TICKET COUNTER IN THE
1950S; RIGHT: EASTERN AIR
LINES STEWARDS IN THE
LATE 1930S; TOP RIGHT: A
TWA PUBLICITY PHOTO;
FAR RIGHT: PASSENGERS
BOARDING AN AMERICAN
AIRLINES DOUGLAS SLEEPER
TRANSPORT FLIGHT.

he came tenth. He was probably the first Edward to be nick-named "Fast Eddie."

When the United States declared war on Germany in 1917, Rickenbacker joined the U.S. Army and, due mainly to his mechanical and engineering capabilities and experience, was offered a position as an engineering officer in a flying training unit at Issoudun in France, where he learned to fly. He earned a place with the renowned 94th (Hat-in-the-Ring) Aero Squadron which frequently engaged Manfred von Richthofen's "Flying Circus." Captain Rickenbacker downed twenty-six enemy aircraft by the war's end—a record for American pilots that stood until World War Two. He had flown more than 300 combat hours: more than any other American pilot in that first great air war.

From 1927 until 1945, Rickenbacker owned and operated the Indianapolis Motor Speedway and made many important improvements, including banking the curves for better, safer cornering. Contacts he had made during WWI led to the business opportunity of his lifetime when he merged Eastern Air Transport with Florida Airways to create Eastern Air Lines. His

stewardship of the airline brought enormous growth and opportunity in the business. He collaborated with some of aviation's greatest pioneers, including Donald Douglas, to help in the development of their products. He frequently travelled for business on Eastern which, by early 1941, had acquired several DC-3s.

He was aboard Eastern's DC-3 Flight 21, from Washington DC to Atlanta, on the stormy night of February 26th when the flight crew contacted their company office in Atlanta shortly before midnight to say that they had just passed the Stone Mountain reporting point and were descending towards Atlanta airport. They then informed the Atlanta control tower that they were two miles southeast of the airport at an altitude of 1,800 feet. They

received clearance to land from Atlanta control at 11:44 p.m. There was no further transmission from the Eastern plane.

Looking out of his window, Rickenbacker saw some lights of the Atlanta Federal Penitentiary through the rain. At that moment he felt the left wing drop as the plane entered a turn—and then it hit something. The left wing came up. Knowing that it was safer to be in the back of a plane in an emergency, he jumped from his seat and rushed down the aisle towards the rear. The plane caught a wing in the tall trees which tore it from the fuselage. Rickenbacker thought of some fellow WWI fighter pilots who, when shot down and facing certain death, had determined to inhale fire to shorten their final agony. He decided he would do the same if the airliner caught fire after the crash. Luckily, the pilots had had the presence to cut the electrical system before the last impact.

The DC-3 had come down in a pine grove near Morrow, Georgia, cartwheeled and come to rest upside down. The wreck was found at 6:30 the next morning. The front third of the fuselage was crushed. Both pilots had been killed instantly. Of the twenty-five persons on the flight, eight—including Eastern's President Rickenbacker who was the most seriously injured—survived the crash. He lay trapped in the wreckage, soaked in fuel and suffering a broken pelvis and hip socket, a broken knee, broken ribs, head and eye injuries. Despite his own terrible condition, he encouraged the survivors to find help and tried to console them and those who lay dying. He heard one of the passengers suggesting that they build a fire to ward off the cold and yelled out to warn them of the danger posed by leaked gasoline from the ruptured fuel tanks.

After many months in hospital and more than a year recovering, Rickenbacker regained his full eyesight and mobility.

Another incident in the history of the DC-3 occurred on the night of February 9th 1937. A United Airlines plane had begun the two-hour flight from Los Angeles to San Francisco at 7 p.m. and at 8:44 the crew could see the lights of the bay area ahead. The weather was good. The highly experienced pilot, Captain Alexander Thompson, was flying the new aircraft, his co-pilot was Joe Decesaro and the flight hostess was Ruth Kimmel. They were carrying eight passengers.

Witnesses on the ground at San Francisco's Mills Field saw the plane cross the field at a height of about 700 feet. It turned out over the bay and continued banking to line up for landing on the east-west runway. It was seen to approach the concrete strip, wheels down, and properly aligned with the runway. They watched as it suddenly and inexplicably fell into a 45 degree dive and crashed behind a large dike separating the field from the bay.

The next day a giant derrick lifted the wreck from where it lay. It was on its back and the fuselage had been torn open. The tail was crushed. The bodies of the passengers and crew were still strapped in their seats. All appeared to have drowned.

This incident took place long before the days of "black box" voice and data recorders and there seemed to be no clues to the cause. Five weeks later, the crash investigators had reached the point of declaring it to be pilot error when something occurred to change their minds.

Another DC-3—this one belonging to American Airlines—was about to take off from Newark Airport in New Jersey. The pilot was running through the preflight procedure, checking the engines and testing the controls for free and full movement. He found they were jammed and was unable to move the control column. Then he spotted the cause. His radio microphone had fallen from its hook and had become stuck in the V-shaped well between the moveable control column and the cockpit wall. He removed the mike and stowed it. Now his control column worked as it should. He took off and completed the flight normally. He reported the incident and all airlines operating the DC-3 were then warned of the possibility of this bizarre event.

The aviation writer for the *New York Herald Tribune* heard about the American Airlines incident and made the mental connection between it and the unresolved San Francisco crash of the preceding February. United Airlines investigators re-examined the cockpit of their wrecked airliner and found the bent, crushed microphone jammed in the control well, as had happened to its counterpart in the American Airlines DC-3 at Newark. The engineers at Douglas learned from the tragedy and designed and installed a leather boot to cover the well of the control column.

By the 1930s, airliners were able to provide faster, cleaner and a less crowded service than the trains of the day. However, flight safety was still a concern for many travellers and potential travellers, and the world media made much of aeroplane crashes. In a campaign to entice more people into the air, the airlines

LEFT: A 1942 MENU FROM THE AVIATION TERRACE RESTAURANT AT NEW YORK'S LA GUARDIA AIRPORT; TOP: AN AMERICAN AIRLINES DINNER KNIFE; ABOVE: A PAIR OF AA KIDDIE RINGS.

CONTROL TOWER
CROYDON AIR PORT

K 1524

.113 BOURGES

Entrée de la Gare de l'Aéroport

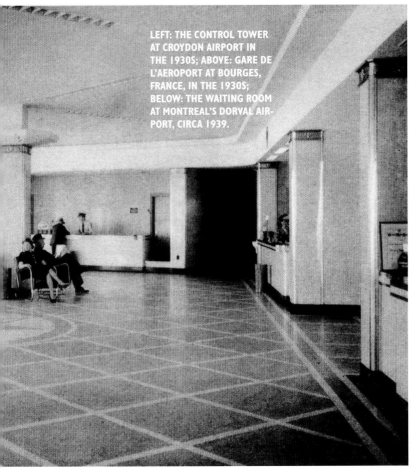

stressed comfort, speed, reliability, quiet and safety in the promotion of their service. Air travel was an exclusive luxury and travellers dressed for the occasion. Since late in the 1920s, airlines, especially in Europe, had given romantic and inspiring names to their aircraft and the route services they flew. Air Union, a French airline, called its Paris-London service Golden Ray, and Silver Wing was the name given by Imperial Airways to its London-Paris service—an important and heavily-travelled air corridor.

In the Art Deco era of the '30s, the people developing promotional materials to bring air travel to the world, rushed to show current and future passengers the technological wonders of the newest, most comfortable and streamlined aircraft. Planes like the Douglas DC-2 were photogenic and stylish.

Convenience was another factor to be promoted in a time when new airports and airline facilities were being developed globally, rapidly and with great enthusiasm. New radio communications systems and a beacon network were being designed, making airline travel at night and in poor weather a reality. Significant improvements in aircraft instrumentation, airfield lighting, and in air traffic control procedures and capability, enhanced the experience as well.

With the advent of the DC-2 and later the DC-3, the travelling public chose to fly on the larger, faster, quieter and more comfortable Douglas airliners, if possible, especially on high-traffic routes such as Chicago-New York. This finally caused United Airlines, America's biggest carrier, with a fleet of Boeing 247s, to accept the inevitable. By the time America entered the Second World War, United was operating a fleet of fifty-seven DC-3s and had relegated its 247s to less-travelled feeder routes.

In general, however, the innovative practices of United Airlines boss, Pat Patterson, kept his company at the forefront in the competition with rivals American, TWA, Eastern, and Pan American. He used such incentives as discounted fares, two-for-one tickets allowing wives to accompany their husbands on business trips for free, new Sky Lounges—a kind of first class service on the New York-Chicago run for a $2. surcharge—and the first in-flight kitchen, bringing airline food to a new and higher standard.

The experiences of the war in the 1940s taught the airlines and the aircraft makers some important lessons about air transport for the postwar years. The pioneering four-engine

Douglas C-54 evolved into the commercial DC-6—an updated model competing with the highly popular four-engine Lockheed Constellation. At the war's end, most of the airlines scrambled to buy and refit C-54s into the DC-4 configuration. Douglas raced to deliver the first of its line of new, pressurized DC-6s. The DC-6 led to the last and largest of the line of sophisticated piston-

engined airliners, the Douglas DC-7—among the first airliners capable of the New York-London trans-Atlantic crossing. The DC-7 came about when American Airlines asked Douglas for a stretched, longer-ranging version of the DC-6. American began service with the Wright Turbo-Compound-powered DC-7 in November 1953. Douglas then developed the ultimate ver-

TOM SWIFT
AND HIS
AIRLINE EXPRESS

BY
VICTOR APPLETON

sion, the DC-7C (Seven Seas) with more powerful engines, more fuel capacity for greater range, and a fuselage extended by an additional ten feet for more capacity. A very refined aircraft, 338 DC-7s were profitably produced. The number would have been higher had it not been for the major airlines' entry into the jet age in 1958.

831—Salt Lake Municipal Airport, Salt Lake City, Utah

NEWARK AIRPORT, NEWARK, N. J. (SHOWING NEW ADMINISTRATION BUILDING)

A view of Peter O. Knight Airport on Davis Islands, Tampa, Fla. — D-10

135—Municipal Airport, Atlanta, Georgia

5—Aeroplane View of Salisbury, Md., showing Chesapeake Airways Transport Plane

**POSTCARDS FROM THE ERA
OF THE DC-3**

Douglas DC-3—Famed for its Record of Dependable Service

227:—OFF FOR A TRIP ON UNITED AIR LINES, LA GUARDIA AIR PORT, NEW YORK

47732

50

La Guardia Field, New York, N. Y.

1B-H2481

111

"When I dipt into the future, far as human eye could see, saw the vision of the world, and all the wonders that could be. Saw the heavens filled with commerce, argosies of magic sails, pilots of the purple twilight, dropping down with costly bales. Heard the heavens fill with shoutings, and there rained a ghastly dew, from the nations airy Navies grappling in the central blue. Till the war drum throbbed no longer, and the battle flags were furled, In the Parliament of Man, The Federation of the World."
– Alfred Lord Tennyson

One of the most repeated quotes about this ubiquitous transport plane is attributed to American General of the Army Dwight D. Eisenhower, Supreme Commander of the Allied Forces in Europe during World War Two, who said: "The four pieces of equipment among the most vital to Allied success in Africa and Europe were the bulldozer, the jeep, the two-and-a-half-ton truck, and the Douglas C-47."

None of them had initially been designed for a combat role.

With the entry of the United States into the Second World War, the U.S. military forces realized that, in the DC-3, they had an important multi-purpose transport aircraft that would be crucial to the Allied war effort. Strangely, it also became the only aeroplane to be operated by every major combatant on both sides in that conflict. Built and flown by both the Soviets and the Japanese, the DC-3—now designated C-47 (among many other variants)—was flown by the Germans in a fleet of aircraft confiscated from various airlines, mainly during the Nazi Blitzkrieg campaign.

The DC-3 acquired a number of nicknames as it took on various guises. When it joined the army it became the C-47 and was called the Skytrain; the C-53 was called Skytrooper by that service. The Japanese-built version was called Tabby by the Allies and Showa L2D by the Japanese. Russia's licensed version was called the Lisunov Li-2. The U.S. Navy version was designated R4D. The military DC-3/C-47 was also referred to as the Gooney Bird, while to the British and Commonwealth nations it was the Dakota or Dak. Vomit Comet was how it was referred to by some of the American paratroopers it brought to Normandy for the invasion of Europe. To Berliners and Berlin Airlift personnel it was the Biscuit Bomber, Candy Bomber, or Raisin Bomber. The search-and-rescue variant was called Dumbo, and in the Vietnam War the AC-47 gunship was called Puff, The Magic Dragon. Other U.S. military members in Vietnam had their own nicknames for it, including Spooky, Dizzy Three, Duck, and Old Bucket Seats, and the EC-47s used there by psychological warfare outfits were known as Bullshit Bombers.

After the mid-1930s it was obvious that another world war was more than just a possibility. The U.S. Army foresaw both the war and its own requirement for a fleet of transport aircraft to take troops wherever they would be needed when that con-

flict came. The army called for bids from various American aircraft manufacturers, including Douglas which proposed to modify twenty DC-2s for the service at $62,000 each, plus engines. Douglas won the contract and the new plane was designated C-33. A further-modified version with better landing gear, brakes, and tail assembly would follow in production called the C-39.

Before the start of the war, General Henry "Hap" Arnold became commander of the U.S. Army Air Forces. Arnold was an old friend of Donald Douglas and wanted to have a better troop and cargo transport than the C-33. He was intrigued by the possibility of creating such a plane from the basic DST/DC-3 and he assigned a team of army engineers to work with Douglas's Arthur Raymond on the development of the army specifications for the C-47. While the C-47 was still in the drawing stage in 1939, orders for it were pouring in, not only from U.S. customers, but from Allies as well. The C-39 was ordered by the army as a stop-gap for a fledgling Air Transport Group until the C-47 was ready. The Group was formed around thirty-five of the C-39s.

The first U.S. Army order for 545 C-47s and 92 C-53s (a major production variant referred to by Douglas as the DC-3A-405 and by the army as Skytrooper) was entered in the Douglas books on September 16th 1940. These were Santa Monica-built civilian DC-3s, differing only in the addition of troop benches, astrodomes, and rifle grommets in the windows. A total of 224 C-53s were built.

Production demands on the Santa Monica Douglas plant began to overwhelm the capability as the company strained to build all the ordered DC-2s, civil DSTs, DC-3s and army C-53s. With the army contract for the C-47, the government built a new facility for Douglas at Long Beach, southwest of Los Angeles. But even this large plant would prove insufficient to cope with the rapidly growing demand for C-47s, and another Douglas plant, at Oklahoma City, Oklahoma, was constructed by the government for additional production of the type. C-47s built at Santa Monica were coded C-53-DO; those built at Long Beach were coded C-47-DL and those built at Oklahoma City were coded C-47A-5-DK. One off-shoot was the C-117—a military executive transport version. 131 of these models were ordered by the army, with the work to be done in Oklahoma, but by the end of the war the contract was cancelled with only seventeen of the planes having been completed.

She's a swell plane-give us more!

MORE PRODUCTION

RIGHT: WOMEN WORKERS IN
DOUGLAS-BUILT BOEING B-17S;
ABOVE: WORKMEN UNPACKING
NEW WRIGHT CYCLONE AERO
ENGINES IN THE DOUGLAS
AIRCRAFT PLANT AT
SANTA MONICA IN 1939.

We Gave

For Home and Country

Baltimore
WAR AND COMMUNITY
FUND

WORK CRAPPY?

JAP HAPPY

BURY the AX in the

AXIS

119

Between 1941 and 1945, Douglas built 9,283 C-47s. These planes were all equipped with a large, two-part cargo door, reinforced flooring to cope with heavy loads, and a slightly up-tilted rear portion of the main cabin floor, to be parallel to the ground when the aircraft was at rest. Standard seating arrangements on the aeroplane consisted of fold-down benches on both sides of the cabin. Some examples, however, were ordered and delivered with conventional airline seats and other airline features. When the troop bench seats were folded down, twenty-four litters could be fitted. A rifle grommet was part of each cabin window. The majority of the engines used in the C-47s were the Pratt & Whitney R-1830, most of them built by the car maker Chevrolet. A few minor distinctions from the DC-3 included a six-inch wider wingspan and a slight reduction in fuel capacity, from 882 to 804 gallons, but the C-47 could be fitted with as many as eight 100-gallon ferry tanks. Most C-47s were built with a glider tow hitch beneath a removable tail cone.

U.S. president Franklin D. Roosevelt directed his Secretary of War to draft all civilian airliners into the Army Air Transport Command (ATC) and the Naval Air Transport Service (NATS) in the week following the Japanese attack on Pearl Harbor, Hawaii, on December 7th 1941. America had joined her British ally in the war and the DC-3 was mobilized and sent into action. Years later Donald Douglas was quoted, "The Gooney Bird was equally at home and equally useful from the Burma Road to Alaska, from New Guinea to Panama, and from the Yalu River to Tasmania; with Montgomery at El Alamein, with Eisenhower at Normandy, in the Battle of the Bulge, and with MacArthur and Kenney in the Pacific. It was unequalled and indispensable."

Operating in all war zones, the C-47 went with the American and British armies, navies, air forces and marines almost everywhere. In the role of air evacuation alone, the plane recovered more than 750,000 wounded from all war theatres.

In 1942, one of the earliest wartime assignments for the Douglas transport was survey flying in order to establish the best routes from the U.S. mainland to England and to the Aleutian Islands. After Pearl Harbor, civil DC-3s and some DC-2s were pressed into service, ferrying troops and equipment, medical supplies and weaponry around the United States, throughout Canada, to Greenland, Iceland, and the Aleutians. Their crews were quick

to prove that the old Civil Aeronautics Board limitations on the weights these planes could carry were far too conservative. They soon set a standard of hauling gross weights of between 29,000 and 31,000 pounds per trip.

When the U.S. went to war, it went mainly by C-47. Among its most vital jobs was the evacuation of 37,000 American and Australian men who had been wounded in combat during the New Guinea and Guadalcanal-Caledonia campaigns in the south Pacific in 1942-43. Naval R4D versions of the plane, flown by Marine pilots from Espiritu Santo, also participated in the Guadalcanal action by resupplying Marine and Navy units there. The Guadalcanal campaign dealt Japan a major blow, seriously compromising her strategic war plan. In surrendering her control of the Solomon Islands, Japan could no longer interfere with Allied shipping to Australia. The key Japanese air base at Rabaul, Papua New Guinea, was thereafter under direct threat from Allied air power. Japanese losses in troops, ships, aircraft and equipment were largely irreplaceable after this first large-scale Pacific defeat. From the end of the campaign for Guadalcanal, the Japanese were forced on the defensive and were never again an offensive threat. The Allied victory had laid the foundation

for the impressive, and ultimately decisive, island-hopping campaigns of the American commanders Admiral Chester W. Nimitz and General Douglas MacArthur.

On the other side of the world, preparations were under way for Operation Torch—the Allied invasion of North Africa and an essential first step towards victory in Europe. This was to be an amphibious landing operation by the British and the Americans, primarily against Algeria and Morocco, which were then under the nominal control of the Vichy French—willing collaborators with France's German occupiers. It began on November 8th 1942. The build-up for Torch included the use of many C-47s, often operating with gross weights of up to 35,000 pounds to bring aviation fuel, paratroopers and supplies to the combat zone from England and Brazil.

The Soviets were pressing for a second front to be opened on the European continent to ease the strain on Russian forces engaged in combat with the Germans in the East. However, British and American commanders were in disagreement. The Americans favoured their Operation Sledgehammer—a landing in Nazi-occupied Europe at the earliest possible date. The British

FAR LEFT: GENERAL OF THE ARMY DWIGHT EISENHOWER, SUPREME ALLIED COMMANDER, EUROPE; CENTRE: IKE'S HEADQUARTERS AT SOUTHWICK PARK, PORTSMOUTH, WHERE THE DECISION TO LAUNCH THE NORMANDY INVASION WAS MADE; LEFT: EISENHOWER TELLING MEN OF THE 101ST AIRBORNE DIVISION, "FULL VICTORY—NOTHING ELSE" PRIOR TO THEIR BOARDING THE C-47S THAT WOULD CARRY THEM TO THEIR DROP ZONES IN NORTHERN FRANCE.

preferred the North African invasion approach. President Franklin Roosevelt broke the deadlock by supporting the British Prime Minister, Winston Churchill.

Operation Torch represented the first large-scale airborne assault by the Americans in the Second World War. The United States' 509th Parachute Infantry Battalion was flown all the way from England in forty-four C-47s to be dropped near Oran in order to capture airfields at Tafarquay and Youk-Les-Bains. But problems with French ground forces over navigation and communications resulted in the drops being widely scattered. In spite of this, the 509th achieved its objectives.

It was the largest invasion in history. It began in the early hours of what the Allies called D-Day, June 6th 1944, when their

soldiers and sailors arrived at the German-occupied beaches of Normandy on the French coast of the English Channel. Delayed for a day due to high winds and heavy seas off Normandy, land forces of the United States, Britain and Canada, supported by Free French, Polish, Belgian, Czech, Greek, Dutch and Norwegian contingents, came ashore at five Normandy beaches code-named Sword, Gold, Juno, Omaha and Utah. More than 156,000 troops and an armada of 6,900 vessels, including 4,100 landing craft, had assembled in English ports in the days before the sixth. The entire operation, under the overall command of U.S. Army General Dwight Eisenhower, had been set for early June when the Allied meteorologists had predicted the required conditions to occur, as well as the essential spring tide and a full moon

FAR LEFT: LEARNING ABOUT THE OPERATION OF THE WACO GLIDER AT A U.S. BASE IN 1944; LEFT: A BRITISH TWO-POUND COIN COMMEMORATING D-DAY; BELOW: A U.S. ARMY WACO GLIDER PILOT READY FOR HIS LAUNCH ON D-DAY.

to aid the aircraft pilots. But the weather would prove less than cooperative.

In the early hours of D-Day, a first wave of 821 C-47s, Dakotas and C-53s took off for France. 800 reached their objectives. 100 C-47s, each of them towing a Waco CG-4 or Horsa glider, made up the second wave of invasion transports, with all but two of the planes accomplishing their task.

The job of many of the airborne units involved was to halt or slow the Germans' ability to organize and mount counterattacks while the landings were taking place. This would enable a sufficient build-up of Allied forces on the beachhead. The key objectives of the paratroopers were the seizure of road crossings, bridges and other features along the flanks of the landing areas, as well as the elimination of German coastal defence batteries.

More than 13,000 American paratroopers, elements of the U.S. 82nd and 101st Airborne Divisions, were flown by twelve troop carrier groups of the IX Troop Carrier Command from airfields in England to participate in a massive and highly risky night drop. It was a tactic that would not be used again for the rest of the war. Nearly half of the units involved ended up widely scattered and were unable to rally once on the ground. After a full day in France, fewer than 4,500 American airborne troops had come under the control of their own divisions, but, ironically, this worked to their advantage by confusing the Germans and reducing the effectiveness of their response to the Americans. The U.S. troops linked up as best they could into small groups from various companies, battalions and regiments; they fought as opportunities presented themselves behind the enemy lines. An early achievement for men of the 82nd Airborne was the capture and liberation of Sainte-Mère Eglise, the first French town to be taken back from the enemy after the landings.

One of the C-47 pilots on D-Day was First Lieutenant Arthur Douglas of New Orleans, Louisiana. "From the moment we were briefed and told this was the real thing, I think all of us wondered just how much there was to the old troop-carrier pilot's joke that 'you train two years for a five-hour job.' Now we were going to find out the answer.

"The paratroopers were something to see as they waited the order to climb into the planes. Some of them seemed very talkative, others relaxed and at ease—just the way they seemed on practice missions. A few of them spent the last few minutes before boarding the plane sharpening a variety of home-made weapons such as spiked brass knuckles and machetes.

"Looking back now, I can say the take-off was routine, one plane and glider lifting from the runway every thirty seconds. But it sure as hell didn't seem routine at the time. This was the mission for which we had spent hours and hours training and gone through scores of practice missions both here and in the States. This one had to be right. If it wasn't it wouldn't be a case of the old man bawling us out. It would mean a messed up mission. It would mean maybe the invasion plan slowed up. Or maybe that the paratroopers would be dropped down where they could do no good and would be easy prey for the Germans.

"I was flying in the third group to go in on our target area. That's a pretty good spot. I was impressed with how peaceful and quiet it seemed as we flew over Britain and crossed the Channel. It didn't seem possible that such a quiet night would be the scene of such a hell of a mess. We kept swell formation all the way over and I suppose everyone—at least the pilots—must have thought 'if the navigation is right, this is going to be a good deal.'

"Just before I gave the four-minute warning to jump—we flick a switch which flashes a green light in the fuselage of the plane and means to paratroopers 'Stand up and hook up'—we ran into the awfullest mess you've ever seen. All hell broke loose. Jerry started throwing lead as if he owned the ground he was protecting. Red tracers arched up lazily and you could see the flashes of the guns on the ground.

"He had our number, all right, because we got hit in our centre section. I knew at the time we were hit that he'd got us, but I didn't know whether it was anything serious. When we kept on flying all right I reckoned we hadn't been hurt. We were about 700 feet at the time, our formation damned good, and even though we could see some planes 'get it' it looked as if we were going to do all right.

"We went over the 'drop zone' in good shape and wheeled for home. Jerry was still throwing up lead and generally making a heel of himself. Naturally, we all dived for the deck after we'd dropped our sticks of paratroopers. We got right down to 100 feet and poured on the coal.

"We were clear out over the coast when our crew chief came up to the cockpit and I said to him, 'How'd it go?' 'How'd it

FAR LEFT: A WORLD WAR TWO SHOULDER PATCH OF THE 82ND AIRBORNE DIVISION; THE DOGTAG OF AN AMERICAN PARATROOPER OF WW2; ABOVE: GENERAL JAMES GAVIN GIVING A PEP TALK TO HIS AIR CREWS AND AIRBORNE PERSONNEL BEFORE THE D-DAY MISSION OF JUNE 6TH 1944.

go?' he said right back to me. 'You still got a plane full of men. Why didn't you give them the green light?' As far as I am concerned I had given them the green light, and I told the crew chief so. He said he'd been back there and the green light didn't show. I tried it and had him watch. It didn't flash, and then I knew that hit we got in the centre section before reaching the signal point had knocked out our electrical system.

"There we were out over the Channel on our way home. We'd been over the drop zone and hadn't dropped. I had to make up my mind quickly whether to continue homeward or turn back and get those guys to a place where they could do some work.

"As far as I'm concerned I'd flashed the green light. And as far as they are concerned I hadn't. What a decision!

"I don't know why, but I turned back. It felt awful lonesome going back there all alone. It wasn't hard to find the way back, but it seemed funny as hell flying all by myself. Naturally, all the Jerrys could concentrate their fire on us, for we were a single plane. Brother, that's exactly what they did. If the first sweep over the DZ had been warm, the second was hotter than the depot stove.

"As we approached the DZ I yelled back, 'Get ready to jump,' and at the very instant we were over it I yelled 'Jump!' The first man to jump was bracing himself in the door ready to pop out.

"Believe it or not, at that very instant he was hit in the middle around which he had his explosives wrapped—maybe hand grenades. He staggered, looked as if he was going to clog the door, so the next man gave him a big push out. It was a good thing for all of us he did, for right then the explosives around him went off and the damned plane jumped and rocked as if it had been shot in the tail by rock salt.

"At first I was sure we'd 'had it.' When the plane responded to the controls I held it on course till the paratroopers had time to drop, then went down for the deck again and started home.

"By this time I felt sure I'd been kicked in the head by a lucky horseshoe. And when the crew chief came up again to say that the explosion had knocked down all the men in their heavy equipment, and they hadn't been able to regain their feet till we'd passed the DZ, I felt like the guy who'd hit the jackpot twice in a row and wasn't due again for another century or two.

"Should I go back again after the men got to their feet or should I go home and make out a 'routine report?' On the second trip over the DZ we'd had our instruments knocked out. I

Canada 49

Juno Beach, Normandy
Plage Juno, Normandie

06.06.44
D-Day · Jour J

had only my compass and air speed indicator and instruments for the right engine.

"I'm telling you that's the time you wished you were back instructing in a school in the States or that you'd gone with the Air Transport Command. There you are sitting like a crippled duck. Nothing to fire back at Jerry with and not even self-sealing tanks or armour.

"Before I knew it I am making a 180-degree turn and heading back for the DZ. Even though I didn't have instruments it was easy to find the DZ by the gunfire—that's where it was thickest. This time we yelled to get ready before we got to the DZ, and when we were over it we yelled, 'Get goin!'

"This time Jerry had everything out and was shooting at us as if the war depended on knocking down just us. It's a wonder a boy with rocks couldn't have knocked us down.

"We all held our breath, I suppose, and after I had waited long enough for all the men to have jumped I stuck my nose toward the deck. And I mean the deck. When I levelled off about 100 above the ground I said to myself, 'I wonder why we're going to have to go back this time?'

"When we reached the coast I turned to see what the crew

BELOW: C-47S OF THE U.S. ARMY IX TROOP CARRIER COMMAND IN ENGLAND, JUNE 1944.

BELOW: C-47S OF THE U.S. ARMY IX TROOP CARRIER COMMAND IN ENGLAND, JUNE 1944.

chief had to say—and I don't believe I'd have gone back again for anything. 'Three of them were either hit by gun fire or knocked out by the bouncing of the plane,' says the crew chief. And I said right then, 'Well, tell them they are going to have to jump tomorrow, for if this crate holds together we're going home right now.'

"The trip back was in the same kind of weather we went out in, and somehow it seemed even more quiet and peaceful. I tell you I felt like a man who'd had a nightmare and knew it was only a nightmare. Some of it seemed awful real, but it was too damned much to be real.

"The three paratroopers we had with us were not seriously wounded and pretty soon they were sore as hell because they didn't get out of the plane and wanted to know why we took so damned long getting to the DZ. I didn't feel up to explaining to them just then why we'd stooged all over Northern France and they were still in the plane. I'd do that tomorrow.

"Half way back I noticed my oil tanks had been hit and I'm losing oil pressure. That's not good. We lose most of our oil on the way back, and when we get over the field and everyone is more or less normal again we find our landing gear on the left side has been shot to hell and gone. We finally get it down and landed all right.

"That C-47 is one hell of an airplane—one hell of an airplane. It can do anything any other plane can do except fly at those God-awful speeds we hear the fighter boys talk about. When we halted on our dispersal we all felt as if we'd had a pretty busy evening and wondered how those paratroopers were doing. It had been only a three-hour trip, but I'm telling you I'd lived a couple of lifetimes."

From *Band of Brothers* by Stephen E. Ambrose: "From May 9 to 12, the 101st held its dress rehearsal for D-Day, code named 'Operation Eagle.' The entire division participated. Easy [Company] used the same airfield it would use on D-Day, Upottery [in Devon, near Exeter]. Personnel and equipment were loaded onto the same aircraft the company would use on the real thing, the take-off, drop, and assembly followed the plan as close to the letter as possible, including spending the same amount of time in flight.

"Climbing aboard the C-47s was difficult, because of all the gear each man carried. Individuals were overloaded, following

AMERICAN AIRBORNE
TROOPS READY TO BOARD
C-47 AIRCRAFT FOR THEIR
PARA-DROP MISSION OF
JUNE 6TH 1944.

DOUGLAS C-47 TRANSPORTS
TOWING WACO GLIDERS
FROM THEIR ENGLISH BASE
TO THEIR LANDING ZONE IN
NORTHERN FRANCE ON
D-DAY; RIGHT: A FRENCH
COMMEMORATIVE MEDAL
HONOURING THE ALLIED
SERVICEMEN WHO TOOK
PART IN THE LANDINGS.

the age-old tendency of soldiers going into combat to attempt to be ready for every conceivable emergency. The vest and long drawers issued each man were impregnated, to ward off a possible chemical attack; it made them cumbersome, they stank, they itched, they kept in body heat and caused torrents of sweat. The combat jacket and trousers were also treated. The men carried a pocket knife in the lapel of their blouses, to be used to cut themselves out of their harness if they landed in a tree. In their baggy trousers' pockets they had a spoon, razor, socks, cleaning patches, flashlight, maps, three-day supply of K-rations, an emergency ration package (four chocolate bars, a pack of Charms, powdered coffee, sugar, and matches), ammunition, a compass, two fragmentation grenades, an anti-tank mine, a smoke grenade, a Gammon bomb (a two-pound plastic explosive for use against tanks), and cigarettes, two cartons per man. The soldier topped his uniform with a webbing belt and braces, a .45 pistol (standard for noncoms and officers; privates had to get their own, and most did), water canteen, shovel, first aid kit, and bayonet. Over this went his parachute harness, his main parachute in its backpack, and reserve parachute hooked on in front. A gas-mask was strapped to his left leg and a jump-knife/bayonet to his right. Across his chest the soldier slung his musette bag with his spare underwear and ammunition, and in some cases TNT sticks, along with his broken-down rifle or machine-gun or mortar diagonally up-and-down across his front under his reserve chute pack, leaving both hands free to handle the risers. Over everything he wore his Mae West life jacket. Finally, he put on his helmet.

"General [Maxwell] Taylor had moved heaven and earth to get enough C-47s for Operation Eagle. They were in constant demand for logistical support throughout the ETO, and Troop Carrier Command came last on the list. It was cheated on equipment. The fuel tanks did not have armour protection from flak.

"Easy got its briefing for Eagle on May 10th-11th. The objective was a gun battery covering the beach. At dusk on May 11th, Easy took off. The planes made 'legs' over England, flying for about two and a half hours. Shortly after midnight, the company jumped. For Easy, the exercise went smoothly, for other companies, there were troubles. Second Battalion headquarters company was with a group that ran into a German air raid over London. Flak was coming up; the formation broke up; the pilots could not locate the DZ [drop zone]. Eight of the nine planes carrying

Company H of the 502nd dropped their men on the village of Ramsbury, nine miles from the DZ. Twenty-eight planes returned to their airfields with the paratroopers still aboard. Others jumped willy-nilly, leading to many accidents. Nearly 500 men suffered broken bones, sprains, or other injuries. The only consolation the airborne commanders could find in this mess was that by tradition a bad dress rehearsal leads to a great opening night.

"On the last day of May, the company marched down to trucks lined up on the Hungerford Road. Half the people of Aldbourne, and nearly all the unmarried girls, were there to wave good-bye. There were many tears. The baggage left behind gave some hope that the boys would be back.

TOP LEFT: A GERMAN GUN BATTERY REMAINING AT LONGUES-SUR-MER; ABOVE: THE MARKER AT THE EDGE OF THE FIRST FRENCH VILLAGE TO BE LIBERATED BY THE ALLIES; ABOVE RIGHT: THE QUINEVILLE CHATEAU USED BY FIELD MARSHAL ERWIN ROMMEL DURING HIS DEFENCE OF THE NORMANDY COAST; LEFT: A GERMAN PILLBOX STILL GUARDS THE APPROACH TO UTAH BEACH; PAGES 140-141: GEOFF LEA'S PAINTING OF A C-47 PARA-DROP MISSION TO ARNHEM IN 1944.

"Training had come to an end. There had been twenty-two months of it, more or less continuous. The men were as hardened physically as it was possible for human beings to be. Not even professional boxers or football players were in better shape. They were disciplined, prepared to carry out orders instantly and unquestioningly. They were experts in the use of their own weapon, knowledgeable in the use of other weapons, familiar with and capable of operating German weapons. They could operate radios, knew a variety of hand signals, could recognize various smoke signals. They were skilled in tactics, whether the problem was attacking a battery or a blockhouse or a trench system or a hill defended by machine-guns. Each man knew the duties and responsibilities of a squad or platoon leader and was prepared to assume those duties if necessary. They knew how to blow bridges, how to render artillery pieces inoperative. They could set up a defensive position in an instant. They could live in the field, sleep in a foxhole, march all day and through the night. They knew and trusted each other. Within Easy Company they had made the best friends they had ever had, or would ever have. They were prepared to die for each other, more important, they were prepared to kill for each other.

"They were ready. But, of course, going into combat for the first time is an ultimate experience for which one can never be fully ready. It is anticipated for years in advance; it is a test that

produces anxiety, eagerness, tension, fear of failure, anticipation. There is a mystery about the thing, heightened by the fact that those who have done it cannot put into words what it is like, how it feels, except that getting shot at and shooting to kill produce extraordinary emotional reactions. No matter how hard you train, nor however realistic the training, no one can ever be fully prepared for the intensity of the real thing.

"General Taylor circulated among the men. He told them, 'Give me three days and nights of hard fighting, then you will be relieved.' Three days and three nights, [Lieutenant Richard] Winters thought to himself. I can take that. Taylor also said that when the C-47s crossed the coastline of France, he wanted every man to stand up; if a trooper got hit by flak, he wanted him to be standing and take it like a man. There was a point to the order that went beyond bravado; if a plane got hit the men hooked up and ready to jump would stand some chance of getting out.

"That night, June 4, the company got an outstanding meal. Steak, green peas, mashed potatoes, white bread, ice cream, coffee, in unlimited quantities. It was their first ice cream since arriving in England nine months earlier. Sergeant Martin remembered being told, 'When you get ice cream for supper, you know that's the night.' But a terrific wind was blowing, and just as the men were preparing to march to their C-47s, they were told to stand down. Eisenhower had postponed the invasion because of the adverse weather.

"By the afternoon of June 5, the wind had died down, the sky cleared a bit. Someone found cans of black and green paint. Men began to daub their faces in imitation of the Sioux at the Little Bighorn, drawing streaks of paint down their noses and fore-heads. Others took charcoal and blackened their faces. 'Nobody sang, nobody cheered, it was like a death march.' Winters remembered going past some British anti-aircraft units stationed at the field, 'and that was the first time I'd ever seen any real emotion from a Limey, they actually had tears in their eyes.'

"At the hangars, each jumpmaster was given two packs of papers, containing an order of the day from Eisenhower and a message from Colonel Sink, to pass around to the men. 'Tonight is the night of nights,' said Sink's; 'May God be with each of you fine soldiers.' Eisenhower's began, 'Soldiers, Sailors and Airmen of the Allied Expeditionary Force! You are about to embark on the Great Crusade, toward which we have striven these many months. The eyes of the world are upon you . . . Good Luck!

143

And let us all beseech the blessing of Almighty God upon this great and noble undertaking.'

"In addition to the exhortations, the jumpmasters passed around air sickness pills. Who thought of the pills is a mystery; why they were passed around an even greater mystery, as air-sickness had seldom been a problem.

"The British airborne had come up with the idea of 'leg bags.' These bags contained extra ammunition, radios, machine-gun tripods, medical gear, high explosives, and other equipment. They were to be attached to individual paratroopers by a quick release mechanism and fastened to his parachute harness by a coiled 20-foot rope. When the chute opened, the trooper was

PAGES 142-143: A CLAYTON KNIGHT ILLUSTRATION OF A D-DAY PARA-DROP MISSION; TOP LEFT: A GERMAN CASE-MATE BEHIND UTAH BEACH; TOP CENTRE: A MEMORIAL MARKER ON A CARENTAN ROAD; LEFT: A GERMAN WARNING SIGN; TOP RIGHT: THE CALM OF OMAHA BEACH IN SUMMER 1994; FAR LEFT: A COPPER MEDAL COMMEMORATING D-DAY.

supposed to hold the weight of the leg pack, pull its release to separate it from his leg, and let down to the end of the rope. It would hit the ground before he did. In theory, the trooper would land on top of the bundle and not have to waste any time looking for his equipment. It seemed sensible, but no one in the American airborne had ever jumped with a leg bag. The Yanks liked the idea of the thing, and stuffed everything they could into those leg bags—mines, ammunition, broken-down Tommy guns, and more. The men threw their kits, parachutes, and leg bags into the waiting trucks, climbed in themselves, and were driven out to the planes.

"Dressed for battle, they sat under the wings of the planes,

LEFT: THE GERMAN WAR GRAVES AT LA CAMBE IN NORMANDY; RIGHT: A MEMORIAL MARKER NEAR CAEN; FAR RIGHT: AN ALLIED LANDING CRAFT ROTTING ON THE BEACH AT ARROMANCHE.

waiting. The nervousness increased. 'This is the jump where your problems begin after you land,' they told one another. It was the '$10,000 jump' (the men had $10,000 G.I. life insurance [policies]). Men struggled to their feet to go to the edge of the runway to relieve themselves, got back, sat down, and two minutes later repeated the process. Joe Toye recalled Lieutenant Meecham coming over to his plane to tell the men, 'No prisoners. We are not taking any prisoners.'

"At 2200, mount up. The jumpmasters pushed their men up the steps, each of them carrying at least 100 pounds, many 150 pounds. One 101st trooper spoke for all 13,400 men in the two airborne divisions when he got to the door of his C-47, turned

to the east, and called, 'Look out Hitler! Here we come!'

"At 2310 the C-47s began roaring down the runway. When they reached 1,000 feet, they began to circle, getting into a V of Vs formation, three planes to each V. As they straightened out for France, most of the men found it difficult to stay awake. That was the effect of those pills. Through the night and into the next day, paratroopers had trouble staying awake.

"At 0100, June 6, the planes passed between the islands of Guernsey and Jersey. In his plane, the pilot called back to Winters, 'Twenty minutes out.' The crew chief removed the door of the plane, giving Winters, standing No. 1, a rush of fresh air and a view of the coast. 'Stand up and hook up,' he

called out. The red light went on.

"At 0110, the planes passed over the coast and into a cloud bank. This caused the formation to break up. The lead V plowed straight ahead, but the Vs to each side veered off, the one to the right breaking away in that direction, the one on the left over the opposite way. This was the natural, inevitable reaction of the pilots, who feared midair collisions. When they broke out of the cloud bank, which was only a mile or two across, every pilot was on his own. Only the lead pilots had the device that would lead them to the Pathfinders' Eureka signals (Pathfinders were specially trained volunteers who dropped in an hour ahead of the main body of troops to set up a radio beacon on the DZ to guide the lead plane)."

"The C-47 pilots had been told to reduce their speed before turning on the green jump light, but, like most of the men they carried, this was their first experience of combat and they too were nervous and frightened. Most felt that the sooner they got out of the situation, the better their chances of surviving were. So, unfortunately for the paratroopers they were about to drop, many of the pilots actually increased their speed as they headed towards the drop zone. As the green lights came on in the planes, many of them flew into severe turbulence. Their drop altitude was less than 600 feet; bright orange tracers from the heavy enemy ground fire added to the scene as 13,400 men of the 82nd and

101st Airborne Divisions lurched to and out of the gaping doors.

Ambrose: "They jumped much too low from planes that were flying much too fast. They were carrying far too much equipment and using an untested technique that turned out to be a major mistake. As they left the plane, the leg bags tore loose and hurtled to the ground, in nearly every case never to be seen again. Simultaneously, the prop blast tossed them this way and that. With all the extra weight and all the extra speed, when the chutes opened, the shock was more than they had ever experienced. Jumping at 500 feet and even less, they hit the ground within seconds of the opening of the chute, so they hit hard. The men were black and blue for a week or more afterward as a result.

"In a diary entry written a few days later, Lieutenant Winters tried to re-create his thoughts in those few seconds he was in the air: 'We're doing 150 mph. O.K., let's go. G-D, there goes my leg pack and every bit of equipment I have. Watch it, boy! J-C, they're trying to pick me up with those machine-guns. Slip, slip, try and keep close to that leg pack. There it lands beside the hedge. G-D that machine-gun. There's a road, trees—hope I don't hit them. Thump, well that wasn't too bad, now let's get out of this chute.'

"Winters had come down on the edge of Ste. Mère-Eglise. He could see the big fire near the church, hear the church bell calling out the citizens to fight the fire. He could not find his leg bag. The only weapon he had was his bayonet, stuck into his boot. His first thought was to get away from the machine-gun and small arms fire in the church square. Just as he started off, a trooper landed close by. Winters helped him out of his chute, got a grenade from him and said, 'Let's go back and find my leg bag.' The trooper hesitated. 'Follow me,' Winters ordered and started off. A machine-gun opened up on them. 'To hell with the bag,' Winters said. He set out to the north to bypass Ste. Mère-Eglise before turning east to the coast. In a few minutes, he saw some figures and used his cricket. He got a reassuring double click-clack from Sergeant Lipton.

"Lipton had landed in a walled-in area behind the hotel de ville (city hall) in Ste. Mère-Eglise, a block from the church. Like Winters, he had lost his weapon when he lost his leg bag. In his musette bag he had two grenades and a demolition kit, plus his trench knife. He climbed over a gate and worked his way down the street, away from the church and the fire. At the edge of town there was a low, heavy concrete signpost with the name of the village on it. Lipton put his face up close to the letters and moved along them, reading them one by one, until he knew that the sign read 'Ste. Mère-Eglise.'

"Paratroopers were coming down around him. Not wanting to get shot by a nervous American, when he saw two coming down close together, he ran right under them. When they hit the ground, before they could even think about shooting, Lipton was already talking to them. They were from the 82nd Airborne, 10 kilometers away from where they were supposed to be. Sergeant Guarnere joined up, along with Don Malarkey, Joe Toye, and Popeye Wynn. A few minutes later, Lipton ran into Winters. 'I saw a sign down the road there,' Lipton reported. 'Ste. Mère-Eglise.' 'Good,' Winters answered. 'I know where that is. I can take it from here.' He set out at the head of the group, objective Ste. Marie-du-Mont."

In the early morning of June 6, a few officers and men of Easy Company slowly approached Ste. Marie-du-Mont. Their weaponry consisted of one bazooka without ammunition, one 60mm mortar, and two light machine-guns. In the grounds of a large farmhouse known as Brécourt Manor, a camouflaged German artillery battery of four 105mm cannon was dug in, positioned to lob its shells on the Allied landing craft at nearby Utah Beach and the warships lying just offshore in the Channel. Winters and the others were ordered to take out the enemy battery.

" . . . the U.S. Army was about to get a big payoff from its training and equipment investment, the American people were about to get their reward for having raised such fine young men. The company . . . that the Army and the country had brought into being and trained for this moment was going into action."

The Allied invasion on the Normandy beaches marked the first successful opposed landings across the English Channel in nine centuries and it was one of the greatest defeats suffered by the German enemy in the war. The new war front was established in France, leading to an improved situation for the Soviets on the Eastern front, and, ultimately, to the final German defeat a year later.

EUROPE AND
THE MEDITERRANEAN

This day is call'd the feast of Crispian: / He that outlives this day, and comes safe home, / Will stand a tip-toe when this day is nam'd, / And rouse him at the name of Crispian. / He that shall live this day, and see old age, / Will yearly on the vigil feast his neighbours, / And say, "To-morrow is Saint Crispian:" Then will he strip his sleeve and show his scars, / And say, "These wounds I had on Crispin's day." / Old men forget: yet all shall be forgot, / But he'll remember with advantages / What feats he did that day. Then shall our names, / Familiar in his mouth as household words . . . / Be in their flowing cups freshly remember'd. / This story shall the good man teach his son; And Crispin Crispian shall ne'er go by, / From this day to the ending of the world, / But we in it shall be remembered . . .
– The King's address to his men before the Battle of Agincourt in France, 25 October 1415. *King Henry the Fifth.*
– William Shakespeare

During Operation Overlord, the Allied invasion landings at Normandy, more than 1,650 sorties were flown by C-47s and C-53s carrying paratroopers and towing more than 500 gliders from bases in England. Assembling and flying in waves of four abreast, they formed an amazing aerial parade between England and France. "The steady stream of transports", reported CBS news correspondent Charles Collingwood, "kept coming and coming in an endless skytrain. The awe of it stopped the fighting in some sectors as men looked skyward with unbelieving eyes."

While D-Day is the best known invasion operation of the Second World War, it was actually not the largest airborne assault of that conflict. That event began on September 17th 1944, when Allied airborne troops made the initial drops and glider landings in Holland. A force of 1,546 C-47s, C-53s and Dakotas, with 478 gliders launched from twenty-four air bases in England, was followed the next day by a second wave of 1,306 transport aircraft and 1,152 gliders. By the ninth day of the assault, 4,242 transport aircraft sorties and 1,899 glider sorties had been flown, prompting General Maxwell Taylor, later Chief of Staff of the U.S. Army, to remark:

"... [this operation] was the best that the division has ever made in combat or in training. Much of the credit for the success of the operation has to go to that old workhorse, the C-47."

The Allied campaign in North Africa was nearing its end and the British and Americans were debating their next major objective in the war. Clearly, they were not yet ready to mount the massive invasion landings in France that would come in 1944. Eventually, they agreed that, with the support of their naval forces in the Atlantic and Mediterranean oceans, their next target had to be the German defences on the Italian island of Sicily. After a thirty-eight day campaign, beginning on July 9th 1943, Sicily would become the first significant portion of enemy-occupied land to fall to the Allies in the war. It would serve as a base for their

invasion of Italy and provide an important learning experience for many British and American officers and enlisted men who would participate in the Normandy landings the following June. The decision to invade Sicily was taken in January 1943 by U.S. President Franklin Roosevelt and British Prime Minister Winston Churchill in a conference at Casablanca, Morocco.

Sicily lies ninety miles from the African coast and only two miles off the Italian peninsula. The operation was to be code-named Husky and the overall effort would combine amphibious landings and airborne drops with glider landings. The goals were to throw the enemy forces off the island, to open the shipping lancs in the Mediterranean, and to contribute to the fall of the crumbling Mussolini government in Italy. The supreme commander of the operation was U.S. General Dwight

Eisenhower. His deputy and designated commander on the ground was British General Harold Alexander and the main Allied assault forces were the British Eighth Army, commanded by Field Marshal Bernard Montgomery, and the U.S. Seventh Army under the command of General George S. Patton.

The operation involved seven army divisions coming ashore along a 100-mile front in the southeast of Sicily. They were supported by elements from two airborne divisions dropped behind the German lines. Four British divisions, a separate brigade and a small commando unit were landed on a forty-mile section of coast from Pachino Peninsula to the port of Syracuse, to be captured in a joint effort by glider-borne troops and the British amphibious forces. In the west of the island, three divisions of Patton's Seventh Army were landed near the Gulf of

Gela, supported by additional American paratroopers.

In the night of July 9/10th, three hours before the main Allied ground forces began coming ashore on the southeast and southwest coasts of Sicily, the first airborne units arrived over the island. Of the four elements involved (two British and two American), the Americans were making their first combat jumps. As they neared the drop zones, strong winds drove the C-47s off course, resulting in fewer than half the U.S. paratroopers reaching their rallying points. The British gliders were also badly scattered and many of them went down in the sea. Roughly one-third of the intercom connections between the C-47s and the gliders failed. The pilots of the C-47s found it difficult to judge the release points accurately and many of the gliders were released offshore. Some of them were diverted by enemy ground fire. Nearly eighty gliders were ditched at sea with the loss of more than 250 men. One glider was shot down and only fifty-four of the gliders made relatively normal landings, with twelve of them reaching their actual landing zones. Fewer than ten per cent of the gliders landed in their target zones. The transport aircraft completed the mission without loss.

Patton's men were overextended in the heavy fighting and urgently needed reinforcements. The general ordered 2,000 more paratroopers from his reserves in North Africa to be dropped near Gela during the night of July 11th. With substantial activity by enemy aircraft over the American sector all day on the 10th, warnings went out to the Allied army and naval units in the area in order to prevent any "friendly fire" incidents where Allied transport planes might be shot down on the 11th. Unfortunately, when the C-47s began appearing over the beaches, a German air raid had just taken place and many over-eager anti-aircraft gunners on land and aboard ship fired on the transports, downing twenty-three and damaging a further thirty-seven of the 144 aircraft. In the wake of the action, it was discovered that word of the impending drop had not reached all Allied units in the area. A nearly ten percent casualty level was experienced by the paratroopers in the action.

Relations and communications between Montgomery and Patton were less than cordial and, when Monty's army became bogged down in its northeastward push towards the vital port of Messina, Alexander directed Patton to halt his own advance to the northwest and move east to protect Montgomery's left flank. Instead, Patton ordered his force towards the capital,

Palermo, later claiming that Alexander's order (via radio transmission) had been garbled. Alexander then ordered an assault on Messina and Patton's army moved into that city on August 17th, a few hours before Montgomery's men reached it and only hours after the last German and Italian troops had left.

In the initial airdrop of the Sicilian campaign, 147 aircraft (including 112 C-47s) towed 137 Waco CG-4 gliders and eight Horsa gliders with a total of 1,600 British airborne troops to landing areas near Syracuse. Operation Husky One followed at night with 3,400 U.S. paratroopers of the 82nd Airborne arriving in 226 C-47s. Jumping in the darkness, most of the paratroopers were widely scattered, once again, and heavy losses resulted. Eight of the C-47s were shot down. The next drop, Husky Two, had more than 140 C-47s bringing paratroops in support of the 82nd. The effort was marred by poor coordination and communications, resulting in twenty-three of the aircraft being shot down and a further sixty badly damaged.

The next drop in the campaign, called Operation Fustian (another disastrous effort), caused the United States Army Air Force to institute the application of what became known as "invasion stripe" markings on all C-47s used in future operations. During Fustian, fourteen C-47s were shot down; fifty more were badly damaged and, of the 132 aircraft dispatched, twenty-seven returned from the mission without being able to complete their drops. In a spectacular event during the Sicilian campaign, one C-47 was so badly holed by enemy shell fire that the pilot was forced to ditch in the ocean. After ordering the jettisoning of all loose gear and preparing those on board for the water landing, he made his descent to the waves. He misjudged his angle of approach and, incredibly, on impact the plane bounced back into the air. Gambling that it was still capable of flight, the pilot coaxed the transport up to a height sufficient for him to nurse it home to his base.

The Allies had learned valuable lessons in the Sicilian campaign that would pay dividends in the Normandy assault. They learned from the inaccuracy of their airborne drops, from their communications and logistical problems, and from their problems with close air support for their ground forces. They certainly learned from their inability to prevent the enemy from successfully evacuating more than 100,000 men and 10,000 vehicles from the island by the end of the campaign. Even so, they had

achieved their main goals in driving the enemy forces from the island and in reopening the Mediterranean sea lanes to Allied traffic. The Germans had been obliged to take military personnel from other war theatres to fight in Sicily. The Italian dictator Mussolini would soon fall, leading to the collapse of the German-Italian Axis and the ultimate surrender of Italy to the Allies. The Americans and British had lost more than 5,500 personnel killed, with more than 17,400 wounded and captured. Enemy dead numbered 29,000 with 140,000 captured. The Germans had successfully evacuated more than 100,000 men from the island. The Allied invasion of Italy followed in September.

Field Marshal Montgomery had devised what he believed to be an ideal plan to shorten the war through an airborne landing near Arnhem in Holland. The plan was code-named Operation Market-Garden and it was relatively simple. Monty knew from his intelligence reports that the closer the Allies came to entering Germany at the Rhine River, the more stubborn the enemy resistance would be. He proposed dropping a large force of paratroopers that would eliminate the German resistance, outflank the enemy defences on the Siegfried Line, assist in the

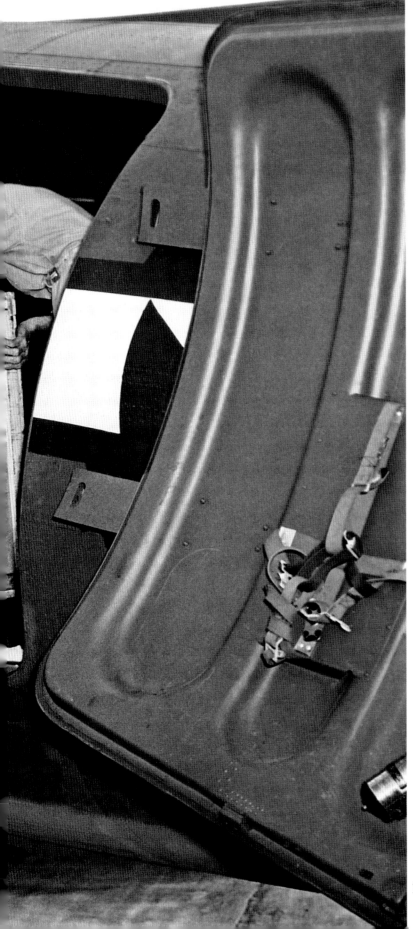

A RESUPPLY FLIGHT IN MASSACHUSETTS DURING 1943.

Allied crossing of the Rhine and attack the German defences beyond the river. Market-Garden was meant to spearhead the British and American forces through Holland and across the Rhine into Germany for the final push towards Berlin. The overall campaign required the Allies to capture five key river and canal bridges and to secure the roads needed for their armoured and supply vehicles.

The Americans, and Eisenhower in particular, were not enthusiastic about Montgomery's plan, believing it would drain away precious supplies and equipment from their own drive towards the Rhine. But when the Germans began launching a new vengeance weapon on London, the V-2 rocket, on September 3rd 1944, Eisenhower changed his mind. The first series of these rocket launches was flawed, but by September 8th the Germans were putting the deadly weapons down on the British capital. In the next few months, more than 1,400 of the big missiles were fired at England, most of them landing in the London area. These attacks continued until March 27th 1945 when the final V-2 landed on the Elm Grove, Orpington, home of Mrs Ivy Millichamp, 34. Mrs Millichamp was the last of 2,754 British civilians killed in the London area by the rocket attacks, with another 6,523 Britons injured.

The V-2 was supersonic. On launch it climbed to a height of fifty miles before its rocket engine shut off. It then arced over and fell silently on its target. British civilians were accustomed to the unsynchronized drone of enemy bombers, the whine of falling bombs, and the sputtering progress of the V-1 flying bomb, but this was something entirely new and terrifying. No sound, no warning—only a devastating explosion.

The Americans accepted that the V-2 launch sites in northern Europe had to be destroyed and that the effort to do so would be made easier with a successful operation in Holland. Accordingly, when Montgomery ran into a stone wall, trying to obtain supplies he needed for Market-Garden, Eisenhower was quick to intercede on his behalf.

It was believed that the strength and morale of enemy forces in Holland were low. The 16,500 Allied paratroopers who jumped into Holland on September 17th 1944 and the 3,500 troops who landed there in gliders soon discovered that their intelligence reports had been spectacularly incorrect. Tanks of SS panzers were awaiting them in Arnhem and the spirits of the German fighting men were, in fact, high.

The order of assignments called for the British First Airborne Division to capture and hold the vital bridge at Arnhem. The American 101st Airborne Division was charged with taking the Zuid Willems Vaart Canal at Veghel and the Wilhelmina Canal at Son, while the American 82nd Airborne Division was ordered to capture the bridges at Grave and Nijmegen. The British First Airborne had not participated in the D-Day landings at Normandy, having been kept in reserve and inactive since June. They were, as their commander, Major-General Robert Elliot "Roy" Urquhart put it: "restless, hungry and ready for anything." Urquhart himself had never before parachuted or participated in a glider landing. He was also subject to air sickness and had expressed surprise when he was appointed to command the division. The commander of the 101st was Major-General James Gavin and the 82nd was headed by Major-General Maxwell Taylor, both experienced airborne combat leaders. In addition to these forces, the Polish Parachute Brigade, under the command of Major-General Stanislaw Sosabowski, had been incorporated into the British First Airborne Division.

The plan called for the Allied ground troops to link up with the airborne troops after the bridges and canals had been taken. The American parachute drops were largely successful with relatively few losses in men and aircraft. Most of the British paratroopers, however, were dropped too far from their objectives and lost the element of surprise as a result. While they did manage to capture the north end of the bridge at Arnhem, they then became caught up in an intense counter-attack by enemy forces there. The outnumbered British troops fought hard but soon came under fire from German Tiger tanks and suffered heavy losses. Further German attacks and deteriorating weather conditions caused a crucial delay in the arrival of British reinforcements, ammunition and supplies, and on September 25th, Montgomery was forced to order a withdrawal from Arnhem. In the disastrous campaign, 1,130 of his paratroopers had been killed and 6,450 were captured by the Germans, whose own killed and wounded were estimated at 3,300.

The operation was largely a fiasco, but the bravery and achievements of some British airborne personnel resulted in the award of five Victoria Crosses and this comment from General Eisenhower: "There has been no single performance by any unit that has more greatly inspired me or more excited my admiration than the nine-day action by the 1st British

THE LAST DANCE BEFORE SHIPPING OUT TO THE EUROPEAN THEATRE OF OPERATIONS IN 1944.

Parachute Division between September 17th and 25th."

Hitler's assault in the Battle of the Ardennes—a last attempt to regain the initiative from the Allies, had failed by January 1945.

By early March the Americans and British had incurred severe losses in men and equipment while fighting their way to the banks of the Rhine. British forces under Montgomery were set to cross the river and secure a bridgehead on the eastern side. From there his infantry and armoured divisions were to move onto the north German plain and into the final phase of the European war.

On March 24th 1945, in the final days of the European war, the Americans and British mounted Operation Varsity, among the most important and controversial actions of the war. Varsity required an immense effort: 2,926 C-47/Dakota sorties to bring more than 14,400 troops and their equipment to the Rhine River—the final barrier separating the Allies from the Ruhr, Germany's industrial centre. In an area between the cities of Wesel and Emmerich, the American 17th Airborne Division and the British 6th Airborne Division needed to capture several important objectives, including road and rail bridges. In this largest and most successful airborne operation in history, the combined forces were charged with securing and deepening the Allied bridgehead east of the Rhine. The German ground forces were clearly expecting the invasion and fought savagely before yielding ground, in and near the drop zones.

Prior to the airborne landings, the enemy propagandist Axis Sally had taunted the American troops: "We know you are coming 17th Airborne Division. You will not need parachutes; you can walk down on the flak."

During the evening of March 23rd, many of the Allied paratroopers wrote their "last letters", to be posted after the impending drop—letters in which they were allowed, for the first time, to tell where they were going. Normally, Company officers had the chore of censoring the letters of the enlisted men. On this occasion, a corporal wrote eleven "last letters", addressed to eleven different women, in which he swore his undying devotion to each one.

In the book, *Airborne At War*, Lieutenant-General Sir Napier Crookenden provides this description of British paratroopers boarding their aircraft at RAF Wethersfield in the early hours of the 24th. Crookenden, a senior airborne commander in the Normandy landings and the Battle of the Bulge, won the

IN THE DAYS BEFORE OTHER ARMY TRANSPORT AIRCRAFT HAD ENTERED SERVICE, THE C-47 CARRIED MANY U.S. AND BRITISH TROOPS TO THEIR DOMESTIC AND WAR ZONE DESTINATIONS; RIGHT: A MEDALLION HONOURING THE LEGENDARY C-47.

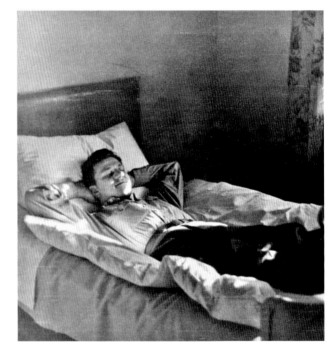

Distinguished Service Order while in command of the 9th Battalion of the Parachute Regiment at the Rhine crossings: "The men climbed in, sat down on the hard metal seats along the side of the fuselage and strapped in. Our American pilots and crew-chief, a senior Warrant Officer, came down the fuselage, talking to the men and checked with me 'I'll give a four minute red, OK?' There was a lot of cheerful backchat and then the engines started. Soon we were taxiing round towards the runway in a long queue to the sound of 160 Pratt and Whitney engines. I was sitting at the aft end of the stick, opposite the open door and had a good view of take-off. Our C-47 turned onto the runway, lined up with two others in a tight V-formation and all three set off together, the two outside aircraft tucking their wings in behind those of the leader.

"Thirty-one minutes later all eighty aircraft from Wethersfield were in the air and forming up into 'nine ship elements', in

FAR LEFT: THE STOLE OF AN AMERICAN PADRE, FOUND ON OMAHA BEACH AFTER THE D-DAY LANDINGS, JUNE 1944; LEFT: SIGN ON ROAD DEDICATED IN HONOUR OF PRIVATE O.A. HAM, 531ST U.S. ARMY ENGINEERS, WHO DIED IN ACTION JUNE 10TH 1944; BOTTOM: AN ENEMY GUN POSITION AT POINT DU HOC, THE SITE OF THE AMERICAN CLIFF ASSAULT ON A GERMAN GUN BATTERY, CASEMATES AND BLOCKHOUSES.

yell of 'Twenty minutes to go' woke us up and sent the adrenalin pumping through our veins.

"We were over the battle-scarred wilderness of the Reichswald and the terrible ruins of Goch, when the order 'Stand up! Hook up!' brought us to our feet. Each man fastened the snap-hook on the end of his parachute strop to the overhead cable, fixed the safety pin and turned aft, holding the strop of the man in front in his left hand and steadying himself with his right on the overhead cable. The stick commander, Sergeant Matheson, checked each man's snap hook, we all checked the man in front and beginning with the last man of the stick shouted out in turn 'Number Sixteen OK!—Number Fifteen OK!' and so on down to myself at Number One.

"Just aft of the door stood the crew chief in his flying helmet and overalls, listening on the intercom for our pilot's orders. I was watching the red and green lights above the door and I am sure the rest of the stick were too. The red light glowed, the crew chief yelled 'Red on. Stand to the door' and I moved forward, left foot first, until I was in the door with both hands holding the door edges, left foot on the sill and the slip stream blasting my face.

"Then the great, curving river was below me and seconds later, a blow on the back from the crew chief and a bellow of 'Green On. Go!' in my left ear sent me out into the sunlight. Once the tumbling and jerking were over and my parachute had developed, I had a wonderful view of the dropping zone right below me. I could see the double line of trees along the road on the west and the square wood in the middle of the DZ. The ground was already covered with the parachutes of the 8th and Canadian Battalions and I could see them running towards their objectives. There was a continuous rattle of machine gun fire and the occasional thump of a mortar bomb or grenade, and during my peaceful minute of descent, I heard the crack and thump of two near misses. It was clearly a most accurate and concentrated drop and I felt a surge of confidence and delight."

American General James Gavin, commander of the 82nd Airborne Division, and flying with the British as an observer above the transport planes, recalled: "It was a new experience to fly an airborne mission, but not jump it. It was an indescribably impressive sight. Three columns, each nine ships or four double-tow gliders across, moved on the Rhine. On the far side of the river it was surprisingly dusty and hazy, no doubt caused

three vics of three, and then into 'serials' of forty aircraft each.

"The rest of the American aircraft carrying British parachute troops took off without incident and on time, except at Chipping Ongar, where a V.1 buzz-bomb caused some excitement as it passed overhead just before take-off at nine minutes past seven. At Boreham, the IX Troop Carrier Command report states, 'emplaning was briefly delayed, while the British finished their inevitable tea'.

"At Wavre in Belgium our column turned to the northeast, on course for the Rhine, and joined the 17th Airborne Division aircraft, coming up out of the southwest. Looking out of our starboard windows I could see their aircraft and gliders stretching back for miles, while from the door on our port side the parachute aircraft, tug aircraft and gliders of our own division from England were still coming up over the horizon. Ahead the two streams of aircraft, each nine aircraft wide, were flying on, side by side, towards the northeast. It was a thrilling sight and a massive demonstration of air power, never likely to be repeated.

"There was some singing in the early part of our three hour flight, but most of the men went to sleep or relapsed into the usual state of half-conscious, suspended animation, until the

by the earlier bombing and artillery fire. On the near bank of the Rhine, clearly visible were panel letters to guide the troop carrier pilots. Yellow smoke was also being used near the panels. It was hard to see how any pilot could make a serious navigational error. The air armada continued on and crossed the river. Immediately it was met by what seemed to me a terrific amount of flak. A number of ships and gliders went down in flames and after delivering their troops, a surprising number of troop carrier pilots we saw on their way back were flying aircraft that were afire. The crew I was with counted twenty-three ships burning in sight at one time. But the incoming pilots continued on their course, undeterred by the awesome spectacle ahead."

Crookenden: "Over DZ 'A' seventy of our aircraft were hit by 20mm shells or machine gun bullets and our 316th Group commander's lead aircraft was hit and set on fire, just as the last man jumped. Luckily the crew were all able to bale out safely.

"Things were rougher for the 5th Parachute Brigade on Dropping Zone 'B'. Here the Dakotas from Boreham and Wethersfield dropped nearly 2,000 men of the 5th Brigade between three and eighteen minutes past ten, but they met a lot of flak. Two aircraft were hit and burning as they ran in, but kept a steady course until all had jumped. In other aircraft seven men got tangled in the strops and failed to jump. As

the tight formation of 315 Group aircraft banked to port and began their turn for home, they ran into intense light flak from the German 7th Parachute Division in the woods near Mehr. Ten aircraft were shot down in the next minute and crashed east of the Rhine and seven came down in friendly territory west of the river. Seventy more were damaged, six aircrew were killed and fifteen wounded in the planes, and twenty were missing.

"The RAF Halifax, Stirling and Dakota crews were briefed to release their gliders over the target area at 2,500 feet, in contrast to the American practice of releasing gliders at 600 feet, and this, coupled with the smoke and dust over the landing zones, resulted in only seven RAF aircraft being shot down and thirty-two damaged. 402 of the gliders were released at the right place, although a few of them were cast off too high at about 3,500 feet. Visibility was down to about 1,000 yards and the glider pilots' difficulties were increased by intense machine-gun and artillery fire from the ground. Ten gliders were shot out of the sky and 284 more were damaged by flak. The gunners on a German 88 on Landing Zone 'P' caused a lot of damage and casualties, as they held their fire until a glider had touched down, traversed round as the glider made its landing run, and then fired, as the glider stopped. Thirty-two gliders were completely

destroyed on the ground and thirty-eight more were under such heavy fire that their crews could not unload them.

"In spite of these hazards ninety per cent of the Horsas and Hamilcars landed on the correct zones and many of them within a few yards of their objective—a bridge, a farm, a corner of a wood, or a crossroads. In the British landings thirty-eight officers and sergeants of the Glider Pilot Regiment were killed, seventy-seven were wounded and 135 were missing. These were heavy losses, heavier than on the first day at Arnhem or in Normandy and might have been heavier still, if some of the American 513th Parachute Infantry had not been dropped by mistake on Landing Zone 'P' and 'R', and if both the American and the British glider men had not run straight from their various touch-down points to attack the German gunners.

"The crews of IX Troop Carrier Command were by now a well-disciplined, highly professional and experienced bunch, and although this particular group was probably one of the best, all of them could fly these tight, precise formations and knew the importance of a steady platform for their jumpers and an accurate and consistent tow for their gliders.

"Each aircrew member wore armour—flak helmet, flak vest, flak apron over the legs and a flak pan to sit on. He was armed with a trench knife and a Thompson sub-machine gun, a car-bine or a Colt .45 pistol and each aircraft carried hand grenades. Most of the C-47s had by now been fitted with self-sealing fuel tanks, but they were still vulnerable to ground weapons, particularly as they ran in to a drop zone or a landing zone on a straight and level course at 110 mph and only 600 feet above the ground. Operation Varsity was the culmination of a lot of flying, and the American orders for it included the recommendation of each serial leader for the American Distinguished Flying Cross and of each aircrew member for the Air Medal."

Operation Varsity successfully opened a northern route through Germany's industrial centre. The cost, however, was high—1,111 Allied soldiers were killed. Among the glider pilots and transport aircraft pilots and crews, ninety-one were killed, with 280 wounded and 414 missing. Eighty aircraft were shot down.

Military historians have argued for years about the relative value of Varsity and the airborne phase of that operation. Some have claimed that it was unnecessary and that British Field Marshal Montgomery was merely "showboating" to enhance his own reputation. Monty denied such claims while asserting that the efforts of his men in driving an additional hole through the German front led to an insurmountable problem for Hitler's forces. In general, Montgomery's position has been supported historically.

RIDING THE HUMP

In 1942, the Imperial Japanese Army had more than one million troops in China. They were opposed by far fewer Chinese forces, whose supply lines extended several hundred miles westward into India through both the towering Himalaya mountain range and the all but impenetrable jungle.

Japanese military forces had invaded China in 1937, successfully occupying and controlling nearly her entire Pacific coast as well as much of the interior. North of India, they proceeded to overrun Burma, seizing the Burma Road in the spring of 1942 and, in doing so, threatening the vital air force units of China and the United States, including Major General Claire Chennault's Flying Tigers American Volunteer Group. The Flying Tigers, so-named by the Chinese, were perceived by many as mercenaries—civilians who had been hired to fight in the air for the Chinese. They were paid $500 to $750 a month and a bonus of $500 for each Japanese plane they shot down. Of the 300 AVG volunteers, 110 were pilots, the rest mechanics and other ground personnel. It being illegal for American military personnel to fight for a foreign power (the U.S. was not yet at war with Japan when the AVG was organized), the volunteers had to operate as civilians. American war correspondent Leland Stowe wrote of the AVG: "Most of them are 100-percent mercenaries, over-cocky and know-it-all. They seemed to have the notion that shooting down Japanese was like hunting squirrels."

These volunteers arrived in Rangoon, Burma, in September 1941, many with their golf clubs and tennis rackets, to be met by the oppressive heat and humidity, awful food, bugs, beetles, spiders, lice, fleas, flies, mosquitos, ticks, bedbugs, and giant rats. From bases in Burma and China, they flew sixty-eight Curtiss P-40 pursuit planes with shark mouths painted on their noses, relying on special tactics adopted by Chennault for combat against the vaunted Japanese Zero fighter. The *Time-Life* correspondent Theodore White wrote: "His squadrons were so mobile they seemed to be everywhere at once. With, maybe ten major centres needing fighter protection, Chennault manages to have his few fighters everywhere they are needed. Chungking and Kunming have not once been bombed since the AVG went into action." At the end of their brief contract period, the Flying

Tigers had accounted for a confirmed 279 Japanese planes downed, with several hundred more probably destroyed. Their operation had been crucially dependent on the same resupply line from India as that of the Chinese.

The Chinese Generalissimo Chiang Kai-Shek was also unable to resupply his armies when the Japanese took control of the Burma Road. His key role at that point was to contain many hundreds of thousands of Japanese troops in a vital holding action in China. American publisher Henry Luce declared: "For $100,000,000 China promised to keep 1,250,000 Japanese troops pinned in the field; to keep Japan's formidable fleet blockading the China shore; to retard the aggressors' march in the direction of U.S. interests. The merchandise was fantastically cheap at the price." Realizing that supplies for the Chinese and the AVG would have to be brought in by air, President Franklin Roosevelt asked the U.S. Congress for the $100 million loan for China as a part of the new Lend-Lease programme, and a further $200 million in military hardware was given to the Chinese. The aid packages for China were intended to build up the strength that the Allies would ultimately need to fight and defeat Japan in Asia and the Pacific, while they were also engaged in attacking German and Italian forces in the European and Mediterranean war zones. To make the Allied strategy succeed, it was essential that China's armed forces be kept supplied in the emergency.

Dramatic measures were called for and immediately instigated by the U.S. Army Air Forces India-China Wing of the global Air Transport Command, in the China-Burma-India theatre of operations. U.S. airmen began flying urgently needed supplies in a hazardous 500-mile airlift through mostly uncharted areas of the Himalayas—a mission commonly referred to as the "Flying the Hump"—to locations in China such as Kunming and Yunnani. The relatively short route was considered to be the most dangerous ever assigned to air transport. From the official U.S. Air Force History: "The distance from Dinjan to Kunming is some 500 miles. The Brahmaputra valley floor lies ninety feet above sea level at Chabua, a spot near Dinjan where the principal American valley base was constructed. From this level, the mountain wall surrounding the valley rises quickly to 10,000 feet and higher.

"Flying eastward out of the valley, the pilot first topped the Patkai Range, then passed over the upper Chindwin River valley,

"The COMMANDO is doing a great job moving men and materiel." — ARMY AIR FORCES

bounded on the east by a 14,000-foot ridge, the Kumon Mountains. He then crossed a series of 14,000 to 16,000-foot ridges separated by the valleys of the West Irrawaddy, East Irrawaddy, Salween, and Mekong Rivers. The main 'Hump,' which gave its name to the whole awesome mountainous mass and to the air route which crossed it, was the Santsung Range, often 15,000 feet high, between the Salween and Mekong Rivers."

The American Hump pilots flew their precious cargoes through dozens of mountain passes at the 14,000 to 16,000 feet levels, far below the treacherous peaks on both sides of their flight paths. Crossing some of the most rugged terrain on

HAMPERED BY TEETHING TROUBLES AT THE START OF ITS MILITARY SERVICE, THE CURTISS C-46 COMMANDO EVENTUALLY BECAME A WORTHY PARTNER TO THE C-47, PERFORMING COMMENDABLY OVER THE HUMP AND ELSEWHERE.

earth, these C-47, C-54, C-87 and C-46 transport pilots brought their unarmed, over-loaded planes through some of the world's worst weather—riding out sudden and violent storms, with heavy snow, rain, hail, fog, deadly icing and high winds. The savage terrain offered little chance of putting their aircraft down safely should the need arise. Some crews flew as many as three such trips in a day.

The Hump air operation did not start from scratch. During the 1930s, important air routes over the Himalayas had been pioneered by the China National Aviation Corporation (CNAC) with the support of the Chinese government and the technical

assistance of Pan American Airways. American Air Force General Hap Arnold supported the CNAC air cargo operation between India and China and soon the U.S. Tenth Air Force, based in India, joined the effort alongside the Chinese. By the end of 1942 the two organizations were delivering a combined 1,000 tons of cargo a month, but this was only a small fraction of the tonnage needed each month by Chiang's forces. Several factors were affecting the operation and limiting the delivery tonnage and these included major shortages in both aircraft and crews. Flight crews were sometimes sent up into the nearby foothills to crash sites in order to recover spare parts for use in the repair of operational aircraft. The planes suffered from poor and insufficient maintenance which often kept them grounded. The frequent terrible weather conditions delayed, curtailed, and cancelled many flights. High-altitude flying conditions played havoc with the aircraft at times, as did the presence of enemy fighter planes, and some Tenth Air Force commanders flying the Hump seemed to lack total commitment to the effort. Thus, on October 21st 1942, General Arnold placed all Hump operations in the charge of the Air Transport Command. He transferred all the Tenth Air Force units flying Hump assignments to the ATC, who employed their new authority and their special air cargo expertise to tackle the problems of the Hump operation.

Airmen who rode the Hump had to fly during the monsoon rainstorms for six months of the year, operating out of the stifling, muggy heat of airfields in India's eastern jungles. The fields turned to muddy quagmires, inhospitable to the men and the planes. Crews lived in perpetually damp clothes, tents and bunks, and those who flew the Curtiss C-46 Commando aircraft also had to contend with soggy, leaky cockpits. In the monsoon season, the combination of driving rain and extreme turbulence near the airfields meant many days of operational delay. The monsoons brought more than 200 inches of driving rain to the ATC bases. But the men persevered and, as some CBI veteran pilots put it: "If you could see the end of the runway through the rain and mist, a take-off was expected."

The launch aircraft of the Hump operation was the proven and reliable C-47—the Army Air Forces' DC-3. Referred to as the "Gooney Bird" by many of her pilots, the C-47 would distinguish herself in every theatre of the Second World War, and in none more so than the CBI. As Otha C. Spencer stated in *Flying The Hump*: "The C-47 was a plane of destiny. No other aircraft in the history of aviation was so revolutionary in its impact on flight. It is an airplane born to fly. To take it into the air is simple—the C-47 takes off on its own. To fly it in the air is not necessary—the C-47 flies by itself. You just tell it where to go and make it behave. To land the C-47 is another thing. You must force it to the ground—it wants to keep flying." The C-47 was the only aircraft flying the Hump operation until January 1943. The C-87, a cargo version of the four-engine Consolidated B-24 Liberator bomber, began arriving in India in small numbers to augment the Douglas transport. The larger C-87s significantly increased the tonnage movement in the Hump flights. Their

ABOVE: CAREFULLY SECURING URGENTLY NEEDED CARGO IN THE MAIN CABIN OF A C-47 TRANSPORT.

seven-ton cargo capacity, combined with the added safety of four engines, a 36,000-foot service ceiling and a 3,300-mile range, brought an improved capability to the mission. But only a few of the ATC pilots had any four-engine experience and, initially, most lacked the necessary confidence in flying the C-87s. It was not until April of that year that the first lot of Curtiss C-46 Commando transports arrived in Karachi to begin service on the Hump run. However, so plagued were they with problems from rushed production, that all thirty of these aircraft had to be flown back to the U.S. for repairs and modification before they could be used in the CBI.

The same thirty C-46 transports returned to India in December. This time they carried huge loads of spare parts and engines. The C-46 had been designed to haul vehicles and equipment too large or too heavy for the C-47, but the C-46 had not been properly tested and quickly showed signs of serious mechanical and electrical faults. Plenty of accidents occurred and many Commando aircrews died as a result. Its flight path across the Himalaya range was nicknamed "the aluminum trail."

The Army Air Forces hoped to replace its ageing C-47 fleet with the C-46. The C-46 came equipped with two Pratt & Whitney R-2800 engines of 2,000 hp each and two-stage superchargers with high and low blowers, making it efficient in the thin air above 20,000 feet. With relatively low fuel consumption, a 200 mph cruising speed and a 15,000-pound cargo capacity, it held great promise, but first the many flaws had to be resolved. Many hydraulic and fuel system problems arose— enough to cause Army maintenance personnel to speak of her as "a plumber's nightmare." In their history *The Army Air Forces in World War II*, W.F. Craven and J.L. Cate stated: "From May 1943 to March 1945, the Air Transport Command received reports of thirty-one instances in which C-46s caught fire or exploded in the air. Still others were listed merely as 'missing in flight,' went down in flames, or crashed as the result of vapor lock, carburettor icing or other defects." Lieutenant General Joseph Stillwell, assigned to the CBI in January 1942 to direct the Chinese ground forces, stated late in 1943: "The C-46 is full of bugs . . . We have lost six over the Hump and the boys' morale is lower and lower." Captain Eddie Rickenbacker, the former WWI flying ace and later head of Eastern Airlines, took on twenty C-46A aircraft for use by his Eastern Airline Military Transport Division. Eventually, after many modifications, the more serious troubles of the plane were identified and fixed. In his testing, Rickenbacker's pilots recommended 517 changes which he reported to General Hap Arnold, who ordered them to be implemented. The aircraft began to earn its place as the new workhorse of the Hump. In time, the pilots and crews even learned to like and respect the C-46. They appreciated it for the visibility and relative comfort in the cockpit, and the power-assisted controls that made the heavy aeroplane easier to handle.

In the capable hands of the ATC, the Hump crews operated in an impressive new climate of efficiency. Many more and better prepared aircraft and personnel were arriving. 100 new C-47A transports and 200 highly experienced multi-engine-rated pilots and co-pilots, along with seventy-five reserve flight officers were sent to India for the airlift assignment. The ATC provided a crew chief/radio operator and a navigator for each of the new crews. Also on hand to provide additional aircrew and support were ATC Army Air Force Base Units, Troop Carrier Groups, Ferry Command Squadrons, Air Commando Groups, the CNAC, Royal Air Force Groups and Royal Australian Air Force Groups and Squadrons. Of the C-47s arriving in the CBI, about fifteen were destroyed or lost on operations, while many of the others spent long periods out of operation owing to shortages of spare engines and parts.

But maintenance improved greatly, as did the quality of weather forecasting. Airfield construction expanded significantly, with more emphasis placed on proper drainage and weather resistance. By the spring of 1943, the goal of delivering at least 10,000 tons of supplies a month to the Chinese armies was re-emphasized by the American president. Franklin Roosevelt was determined to increase U.S. support for the Chinese ally. In line with this intensified effort, thousands of workers and an enormous amount of building equipment were soon diverted from road construction to the new airfields. In the next two years, nineteen air bases were completed in India and China for the ATC. Much of the actual construction work was done by Chinese civilian labour—men, women and children—in tens of thousands. They took rocks brought to the sites on ox carts and broke them up, using crude picks to turn them into small chips that were compacted by primitive stone-filled rollers into bedding for the new landing strips.

Life on the ATC air bases in the CBI was miserable for the air-

RIGHT: FAR EAST COMMANDER GENERAL DOUGLAS MACARTHUR; BELOW: A BULLION JACKET PATCH OF THE CBI BURMA BRIDGE BUSTERS.

RIGHT: A TYPICAL PRE-FLIGHT SCENE IN THE TROPICS, A C-47 WAITS ON A PIERCED STEEL PLANKING SURFACE AS PERSONNEL SHELTER IN THE SHADE OF THE WING; BELOW: MUCH OF THE HUMP FLYING WAS OVER DENSE, THREATENING JUNGLE TERRAIN.

crews. Despite the best efforts of the ATC, the persistent short-ages of major and minor items could not be resolved. Morale was dangerously low, but the airmen who, as one put it, were "living like dogs and flying like fiends," did the job. They even started a spirited competition—attempting to load more cargo and to complete more missions than the others in their units, while accruing the most flying hours and the fewest accidents. However, a lot of accidents did occur—some unavoidable—and many airmen and aircraft were lost in the pursuit of the 10,000-tons a month goal, finally achieved in December 1943. The pilots and aircrew had too little time on night-flying ops, and flying heavily-loaded transports in extreme weather at high altitudes carried a very high fatigue factor. The ATC suffered 155 major aircraft accidents during the second half of 1943 and 168 air-crew fatalities flying the Hump.

The crews were flying more than 100 hours a month. Many pilots had no prior twin-engine aircraft experience, having been recruited as basic flying school instructors in Air Training Command. With spare parts hard to come by, and maintenance personnel inexperienced, it was little wonder that the accident rate was high. Colonel Edward Alexander, then commander of the India-China Wing, commented at the time: "Except on rainy days, maintenance work cannot be accomplished because shade temperatures of from 100 degrees to 130 degrees Fahrenheit render all metal exposed to the sun so hot that it cannot be touched by the human hand without causing sec-ond-degree burns."

During the war, American Airlines president, Cyrus R. Smith, took a leave of absence to serve as a major-general with the U.S. Air Transport Command where he was most effective as a trouble-shooter. He visited the CBI late in 1943 to observe and report on the airlift conditions and on the many accidents in the pro-gramme. Smith: "We are paying for it in men and airplanes. The kids here are flying over their head—at night and in daytime—and they bust [the aircraft] up for reasons that sometimes seem silly. They are not silly, however, for we are asking boys to do what would be most difficult for men to accomplish; with the expe-rience level here, we are going to pay dearly for the tonnage moved across the Hump . . . with the men available, there is nothing else to do."

With time, operational experience and the addition of more crews and aircraft, though, both the safety factor and the tonnage

hauled improved dramatically. Supplies carried rose to 15,000 tons a month by spring 1944. By the end of the year, the aver-age tonnage carried had risen to 34,000. The goods were being delivered to the Chinese with efficiency, but the accident rate was still too high and morale among the airmen still too low.

In an effort to improve the operation further, a new com-mander was brought in to take charge of the Hump flying. Brigadier-General William H. Tunner was a disciplined, no-nonsense West Point graduate who became the outstanding U. S. Air Force authority on airlift operation. In 1948 Tunner was chosen to direct the giant Berlin Airlift, when the Soviets block-aded all land and sea supply routes to the German city. Tunner: "It seems almost incredible that up until three o'clock in the afternoon of May 29th, 1941, there was no organization of any kind in American military aviation to provide for either delivery of planes or air transport of materiel."

In September 1944, it was Tunner's task to increase operational efficiency, improve safety in the Hump flight operations, and to raise morale. He began by insisting on an improvement in the appearance of his personnel, with appropriate military dress and attention to detail. He raised the standard of meals and recreation opportunities, while implementing more accu-rate weather forecasting and better aircraft maintenance. A highly-qualified, grimly determined hands-on leader, General Tunner took the controls of a C-46 Commando transport on a typical trip over the Himalayas from an Indian base to see for himself the sort of conditions faced daily by his crews. He noted the numerous blackened blotches along the runway—evidence of ATC transports that had crashed and burned while trying to fly the Hump missions—and resolved to lower the accident rate. By the end of the Pacific war, he had succeeded in cutting that rate by half. Tunner: "Every drop of fuel, every weapon, and every round of ammunition, and 100 percent of such diverse supplies as carbon paper and C-rations, every such item used by American forces in China was flown in by airlift." He noted the cost in American lives: "It was safer to take a bomber deep into Germany than to fly a transport plane over the Rockpile from one friendly nation to another."

The innovative Tunner instituted a system of production line maintenance to improve the safety and operational availability of his planes. Aircraft due for routine maintenance passed through as many as ten work stations. Different maintenance procedures were performed at each station and all of the completed work was thoroughly inspected at the end of the line. When the work passed inspection, the aircraft was test-flown before being returned to operations. The success of Tunner's line maintenance approach was so impressive that it soon became standard practice throughout the Army Air Forces. His interests didn't stop at the aircraft.

Tunner received reports from his flight surgeon that nearly half of the pilots flying the Hump were suffering from operational fatigue—a condition frequently leading to flying accidents. Many pilots were so anxious to finish their Hump tours and go home, that they were flying as many as 165 hours a month to accumulate the flight time required as fast as possible. On learning of the practice, Tunner immediately changed the policy to make his pilots fly in the CBI for one full year and for 750 flying hours, before they could go home. While the change did not increase his popularity, it did save lives and, in the end, the pilots were grateful to him.

One troubling affliction for many of the airmen was the

AMERICAN NURSES TAKE A BRIEF BREAK FROM PATIENT DUTIES AT A PACIFIC AIR EVACUATION BASE.

"Dhobi itch," a persistent and nasty form of rash common in the climate. They lived, too, with the threat of malaria, which required them all to take a daily dose of Atabrine—a yellow tablet available on the mess hall tables along with the salt and pepper. The Atabrine helped in the fight against malaria, and to improve the living conditions of his men still further, Tunner established a programme of aerial spraying to help repel the malarial mosquitos in the region. He employed stripped-down North American B-25 Mitchell bombers that he called "Skeeter Beaters". These, in combination with the Atabrine and the use of mosquito netting and repellents, proved effective in reducing the incidence of malaria among his personnel. Tunner: "I had been sent to this command to direct American soldiers and while I was their commander, by God, they were going to live like Americans and be proud they were Americans."

Before Tunner's arrival, an early form of search-and-rescue organization had been set up to cope with the problem of helping airmen who had been forced to bail out or crash-land in the harsh terrain, to get to safety. Survival could be down to a matter of a few days, or even hours, and movement for downed, ill, injured or burned airmen was difficult. In the first months of the Hump flying, news that one of the planes had gone down sent the first available crew and aircraft off on a search for the missing airmen. Later on, Chabua-based Captain John "Blackie" Porter organized Blackie's Gang—two C-47s and crews armed with .30 calibre machine-guns, Tommy guns and hand grenades. Porter's outfit was successful in several search-and-rescue efforts and he was later placed in command of a more formalized search-and-rescue unit. He was lost in action on such a mission in December 1943.

William Tunner quickly focused on the need to strengthen the search-and-rescue capability and appointed Major Donald Pricer, one of the Hump pilots, to command the SR unit. Four B-25s, a C-47 and an L-5 spotter plane were painted a bright yellow and assigned to the new unit with the job to locate and identify all aircraft wrecks in the area, in order to eliminate confusion and duplication of effort. In another related move, Tunner ordered that a jungle indoctrination camp be established at each of his bases, with attendance compulsory for all new arrivals.

In his tenure with ATC, Tunner's cargo aircraft inventory grew

U.S. MILITARY PERSONNEL RECOVERING IN A NISSEN HUT BASE HOSPITAL AT DIDDINGTON, ENGLAND. THE MOST SERIOUS CASES WILL BE EVACUATED BY AIR TO STATESIDE FACILITIES FOR MORE ADVANCED CARE.

from 369 to 722 and his personnel from 26,000 to 84,000. By the final phase of his operations to and from China, one ATC transport aircraft was taking off every three minutes and the monthly cargo deliveries reached an average of 44,000 tons, peaking in July 1945 at a massive 71,000 tons. More than 650,000 tons of gasoline, munitions, men and materiel had been flown over the Hump during the airlift. The operation far exceeded the supply requirement of the Chinese and made it possible for the troops of Chiang Kai-Shek to tie-up more than a million soldiers of the Japanese Imperial Army in China. This seriously limited the fighting personnel available to Japan for opposing the Allied amphibious landings in their Pacific island-hopping campaign, and shortened the war. The official Air Force History: "Here [in the CBI], the AAF demonstrated conclusively that a vast quantity of cargo could be delivered by air, even under the most unfavourable circumstances, if only the men who controlled the aircraft, the terminals, and the needed materiel were willing to pay the price in money and in men." General William H. Tunner: "For every thousand tons flown into China, three Americans gave their lives."

The highly regarded journalist and war correspondent Eric Sevareid wrote of a trip he made with a C-47 crew on a re-supply mission over the Hump: "That day there was not a cloud in the skies over North Burma, and that was bad. The Japs liked to catch unarmed transport planes like ours, flying 'over the hump' between China and India, and the radio operator had just reported that four Zeros were somewhere around.

"Teetering on a wooden ration box, I thrust my head up into the glass bulge on the top of the C-47, peering into the dazzling blue for signs of the Zeros. I could see a long distance in three directions over the greenish, jungle-covered hills, but when I gazed eastward, toward the China we had left an hour before, the morning sun blinded me. If we could spot the Zeros first, we had a chance. The pilot, Lt. George Hannah of Louisville, could slip the camouflaged plane down low into the valleys and try to sneak away. But if they saw us first and came at us out of the sun—well, another plane number would probably be rubbed off the blackboard in the operations shack at the Assam base in India; and the boys who regularly fly the hump into China would say, in that misleadingly casual tone I have heard so many times, 'Hannah got his today.'

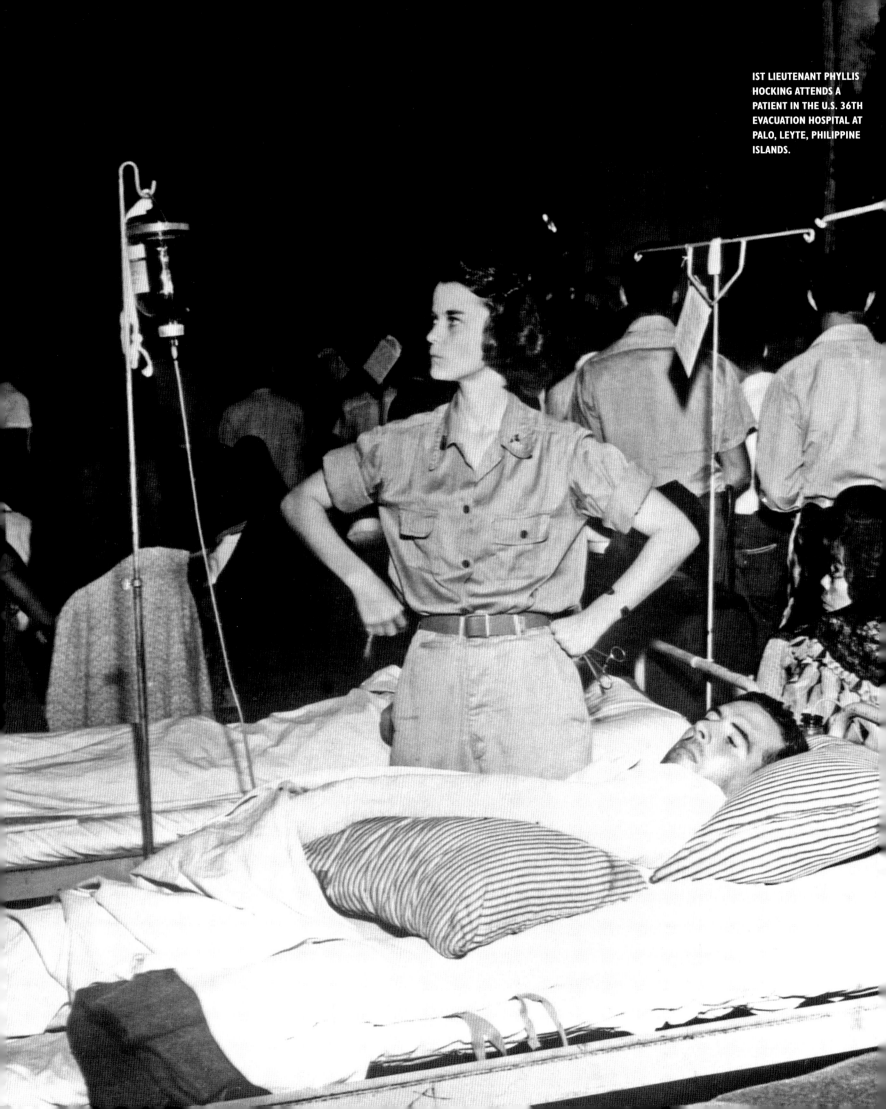

IST LIEUTENANT PHYLLIS HOCKING ATTENDS A PATIENT IN THE U.S. 36TH EVACUATION HOSPITAL AT PALO, LEYTE, PHILIPPINE ISLANDS.

"The crew chief took my place and I stood behind the pilots, watching the ridges lapping toward us. The co-pilot, who had not made this run often, was a little nervous and would quietly suggest to Hannah that maybe we wouldn't clear the next one, a quarter-mile away. Hannah would say nothing, but turn and wink at his colleague as we cleared the ridge with no more than 40 feet to spare. That was the idea; on a cloudless day it was no good flying high, because that's where the Zeros played about. Instead, you just coasted over the hills, below the horizon of the next range, risking a sudden downdraft which might smash you, but making it tough for the Zeros to pick you out in the bewildering patterns of green and brown.

"There was another risk. Hannah pointed down to a cluster of long, low, wooden buildings, thatched with palm and banana leaves. We were flying directly over some Japanese army barracks, almost within pistol range. I cannot describe the sensation it gave me; I know the meaning now of the phrase, 'between the devil and the deep blue sea.' We stared at the brush below, waiting for the first machine-gun tracer bullets. Hidden machine-guns on the North Burma hillsides have downed more than one of our transport planes.

"But this time there was no shooting. We roared on and suddenly, dead ahead, we saw a narrow, white gash winding across the hills. This was the 'Ledo Road' which American army engineers are driving through toward its ultimate connection with the old Burma Road. We were over it in a moment and knew then that we had the protection of our own anti-aircraft guns hidden somewhere in that impenetrable bush below us. In a little while our three-hour run from China was ended and we stepped out into the muggy heat of Assam. I never felt more relieved in my life and even Hannah, I noticed, was mopping the sweat from his ruddy face. He had that day completed his 96th flight over the hump.

"Hannah is just one of hundreds of American boys who have been 'sweating it out' over that route for the last two years. They are carrying gas, bombs and ammunition for Major General Chennault's 14th Air Force, and jeeps, guns, medicine and a thousand other items to keep China's flickering resistance alive. They have helped to hold the great bastion of the Chinese earth where one day, Lieutenant General Stillwell believes, Japan's ultimate fate may be decided.

"Strangely assorted cargoes have been carried back out of China: ingots of tin ore and wolfram for America's factories;

American soldiers on stretchers, some silent with wounds, others twisting and turning, racked with malaria; Chinese soldiers sent to India for training with modern American weapons, under American officers. These Chinese troops will go back into China on foot, fighting their way. Some are already doing so, clearing the Japs away from the advancing Ledo Road.

"Few Americans know the story of the great hump flight, because the War Department had to maintain silence until now. Today the story can be told, because our protection of the route is more complete.

"We have a long list of unsung heroes in this war, and the Air Transport Command youngsters who have flown the hump day in and day out ought to be placed near the head of this list. Most of them haven't even been able to let their families know what they are doing. 'Just flying a routine transport run'—it sounds at a distance like a cinch, but I have heard our fighter pilots and bomber crews out there talk about the hump flyers, and I know the deep respect in which they are held. I remember Lt. Tommy Harmon, who fights in a P-38, saying at mess: 'I would rather fly a fighter against the Japs three times a day than fly a transport over the hump once.'

"The ATC operations room is like a combat headquarters. Every night, when I was there, they jotted down the casualties or near-casualties for the day. It takes a particular type of lad to fly this route. His navigation must be excellent, because for most of the three-hour run he must maintain radio silence, and it is very easy to get lost over that rugged terrain, especially if he must fly among the towering ice-covered peaks which extend eastward from the principal range of the Himalayas.

"He must know his plane thoroughly and how it will react in all kinds of weather. He may leave India deciding to fly low over the Burma hills and find that an unforeseeable monsoon storm forces him up to 18,000 feet, where his plane may ice over in a few moments. If he has passengers, the crew chief must revive those who pass out for want of oxygen.

"Most of all, he must have steady nerves. The brash, highly strung boy who makes a good fighter pilot will not do. To be attacked when you have a gun in your hand is one thing—anybody feels confident. But to know that a Zero is after you and that you are utterly defenceless, and still to keep your eyes ahead and your mind working logically to figure out your escape—that is something quite different.

"Planes crack up on the hump, and so do flyers. Expert medical officers, such as Col. Don Flickinger at the India base, examine the pilots at frequent intervals; at the first sign of fraying nerves they are sent out for a rest—to the luxuries of Calcutta, or the

RIGHT: AIR EVACUATION PATIENTS WAIT ON STRETCHERS BENEATH THE WING OF A C-47 IN ITALY; FAR RIGHT: RELAXING WITH A SMOKE ABOARD A C-47 EVACUATION FLIGHT.

cool lakes and pines of Kashmir. Some, like Hannah, seem to go on forever without a break in their nervous systems, but they are not many.

"Those who complain that we are 'doing nothing for China' would be surprised at the amount of stuff we are delivering by air over the hump. There are scores of flights into China every day in the year. The Burma Road, at its very peak, carried about 15,000 tons of supplies into China per month. My guess is that the ATC is already approaching that figure. Of course, that is pitifully little. One big cargo ship a month would equal it.

"Sitting about the barrack rooms you hear constant talk of crew members who are 'hiking out.' Boys who have had to bail out of their plane somewhere on the hump are trying to find their way across the ridges and through the jungles to the India or China side. I have heard endless discussions among the flyers as to what they would do if their turn came, what equipment they would try to salvage, where they would head for. It is constantly on their minds. They study carefully their excellent large-scale maps, noting the little red circles which indicate positions held by the enemy.

"The record of rescues is getting better, partly because more head-hunting natives are learning that rewards of salt and cloth await them if they find and return the boys unharmed. And we have more crews now which do nothing but nose their C-47s day after day through the innumerable valleys, looking for a fluttering bit of white cloth which may be the signal of a lost American flyer. More and more boys are turning up, brought by horse-cart into China (Chinese peasants are quick to hide them from the Japs) or

led into India by Naga natives.

"I know how efficient the rescue work can be, once the search plane spots you on the ground. Flying over the hump last August, the plane I was in developed engine trouble and the 20-odd of us aboard had to bail out into the jungle. It took us 27 days to get out.

"There are many stories of far worse experiences. You cannot crash-land your plane on the hump because there isn't a level, cleared spot to be found, but two American boys once managed to land on the side of a snow-covered peak, and lived. Both suffered broken ankles. They huddled in the wrecked airplane, eating their scanty canned rations, wrapping themselves in their parachute silk for warmth. Several times searching planes flew near but all their signalling was in vain.

"When their food was nearly gone, they bandaged one another's ankles and stumbled and slid down the mountain. Only one who has tried to walk on a broken bone can imagine what they went through. By a stroke of luck, wandering Chinese discovered them one day, lying by a stream, without strength to go on, and nineteen days later they were safe in an Air Force hospital.

"It would not be honest reporting to ascribe all the troubles and tragedies on the Hump to the enemy and the elements. Among the transport planes used was a new model [the C-46], hurried into service because of popular pressure in America for more aid to China. Fundamentally, it is a superb airplane, but it was very new then and all the 'bugs' in it were by no means ironed out. This model hauled many hundreds of tons of supplies into China, but a good many of the planes crashed and lives were lost. In time, these planes are expected to be as reliable as the steadfast C-47."

RIGHT: A REAL-LIFE NELLIE FORBUSH, ALA THE RODGERS AND HAMMERSTEIN MUSICAL, 'SOUTH PACIFIC', WASHING THAT MAN RIGHT OUT OF HER HAIR; BELOW: A FRIENDLY GAME FOR MATCHSTICKS; FAR RIGHT: THE QUEUE FOR A FIELD SHOWER, ROUTINE FOR THESE U.S. ARMY NURSES ON A PACIFIC ISLAND IN WORLD WAR TWO.

ANOTHER PACIFIC QUEUE, FOR CHOW HAPPILY SERVED BY SOME ENTHUSIASTIC G.I. COOKS TO THESE AMERICAN NURSES IN HAWAII; FAR RIGHT: 'OPPRESSIVE AND BRUTAL' IS HOW THE U.S. ARMY FLIER IS PORTRAYED IN THIS JAPANESE PROPAGANDA POSTER OF WORLD WAR TWO.

There is a theory that the practice of decorating the fronts of military aircraft derives from the nautical tradition of figure-heads on the sharp ends of sailing vessels—frequently shaped as large-breasted, scantily-clad females. Psychology professor and World War Two B-17 navigator, George Klare, wrote of the phenomenon in *The History of Aircraft Nose Art* by Jeffrey L. Ethell and Clarence Simonsen: "Sexual deprivation, or at least diversion, clearly played a major role in nose art as in earlier sea art, true. But did sex as such provide the underlying reason for nose art? The picture does not seem all that clear.

"My own view is that the psychological mechanism of identification was a more inclusive reason for nose art. Crew members on the sea or in the air wanted to see their complex ships as almost human entities with which they could identify. Especially when they faced danger, they even wanted to endow their ships with almost superhuman qualities to protect them and bring them safely back. Certainly many references made by combat crewmen to the B-17 (with which I am most familiar) carried that kind of connotation. The nicknames 'Flying Fortress' and 'Queen of the skies' were the most common. Recall too that Charles Lindbergh's story of his solo crossing of the Atlantic was titled *We*. This need to identify with a ship also appeared among ground crew, who felt a strong sense of responsibility for the safe performance of their airplane and sweated out missions along with the air crew.

"Equally if not more important, nose art and names made it possible for airmen to identify somewhat more readily with each other and feel pride and confidence as a crew. Developing strong relationships among crew members was always a goal in air crew training. In fact, when a particular crew member did not get along well with, or have the confidence of, the rest of the crew a transfer often resulted. Members of a combat crew needed to depend on each other, and identification with their airplane helped to create strong interdependence among crew members. The crew itself also replaced home security influences in some cases, and afforded a bulwark against homesickness. Some members of these young crews found themselves away from home for the first extended stay in their lives, and for the first time faced death directly and personally.

"Superstitious behaviour consequently became another aspect of identification. Just as professional athletes do, air crew members often had rituals meant to bring good luck or, more

important in combat, ward off bad luck. For example, a member of my crew regularly put his chewing gum alongside the rear door of our B-17 just before we began a mission. After we were shot down, he lamented not having done so that day.

"The choice of fierce or protective names or paintings seems to be part of this sort of ritual, as can be seen in the kinds of four-legged animals and even six-legged insects chosen.

"Occasionally one of these designations either had, or grew to have, an unlucky connotation, and air crew members were known to shun such an airplane and dread having to fly in it. Logic dictated that chance played a major part in a bomber crew's survival in combat, but emotion often made such lack of control unacceptable. Superstitious behaviour involving a favourite airplane seemed to mean good luck, at least until a fatalistic attitude developed."

THE BIG LIFT

LEFT: CHILDREN OF BERLIN WAVING TO SHOW THEIR GRATITUDE TO THE CREW OF A C-47 SKYTRAIN FOR THE FOOD, FUEL, AND THE OTHER DESPERATELY NEEDED SUPPLIES FLOWN INTO THE CITY EACH DAY DURING THE 1948-1949 AIRLIFT OPERATION.

It began officially at midnight on June 23rd 1948, and ended at 5:32 a.m. on May 12th 1949: one of the greatest events in aviation history. The Berlin Airlift.

Authors Ann and John Tusa wrote a book in the 1980s called *The Berlin Airlift* which was published in 1988. Ten years later, Ann gave a talk on the Airlift to an audience at London's Imperial War Museum. Here, courtesy of the Tusas, is the text of her compelling lecture: "Imagine yourselves sixty years ago. It's 24th June 1948 and you are in West Berlin. Last night, soon after midnight, all the electricity went off. Most of it came from Soviet-controlled power stations and the Russians have cut the supply. A few generators are now struggling to provide emergency supplies but the Underground and the metropolitan surface railway are not working. Nor are the buses—the city is about to run out of petrol and doesn't expect to get any more. No one has told you that there are only stocks of coal in West Berlin for forty-five days, but you know perfectly well that no more coal can get into the city—the Russians won't let it—so light, heating, anything using electricity is soon going to stop. You panicked this morning and filled the bath, the basins and every bucket, pan and jug in the house with water. Then the radio told you to calm down and use as much water as you want; 'there are ample reserves' it said. Yes, there is plenty of water, but it comes from deep wells and has to be pumped out electrically. You have queued all day for food. Any food. Because none got into the city today and none is expected—the Russians have cut the road and rail communications which brought it. There have been radio broadcasts all day telling you not to hoard, because there is food in store for the 'immediate future'. But how long is that? The Town Hall knows—there are stocks for thirty-five days. They put them under lock and key today while they worked out rations to stretch those meager quantities. Tomorrow you'll find there is not a single pint of fresh milk available; if you ate fresh vegetables or fruit today, they may have been your last for eleven months. You're under siege.

"You're not really surprised by any of this. For months now you have been dreading a crisis. You've known that a major international confrontation has been simmering and that it would come to a boil in Berlin.

"Since the end of the Second World War in May 1945 Germany has been under military occupation by the four leading members

AT TOP FROM LEFT: KEY
PLAYERS IN THE BERLIN AIR-
LIFT, GENERAL CURTIS
LEMAY, MAYOR ERNST
REUTER, AND GENERAL
WILLIAM TUNNER; ABOVE:
NIGHT OPERATIONS IN THE
AIRLIFT AT TEMPELHOF.

of the coalition which defeated Hitler—the Soviet Union, United States, Britain and France. They have divided the country into four zones, set up their government, the Allied Control Council, in Berlin and divided the city into four sectors. Berlin, however, is inside the Soviet Zone of occupation; it is over 100 miles by direct road or rail from the western zones. In the first chaotic weeks after the end of the war, the Russians said they did not have transport to carry supplies and their own zone was starving. They persuaded their western allies to take responsibility for providing three quarters of the food and fuel for the three western sectors of Berlin. To carry these supplies, the Russians only conceded one road, one railway line and a few canals from West Germany. The western allies hadn't argued: they were too appalled by the devastation they faced in Germany, too anxious to get Soviet cooperation in running the place. Anyway, they assumed these ludicrously inadequate arrangements were only temporary and they could renegotiate them once four-Power government was set up. Indeed, Field Marshal Montgomery recalled in 1948: 'we thought we had a gentleman's agreement and that everyone would do his stuff.' Well, the Russians were never gentlemen in Germany, the stuff they wanted to do there was very different from western ambitions. So, the traffic rules for the western sectors were never changed. The vulnerability of one road, one railway line from the West through a hundred miles of Soviet-held territory made two and a half million West Berliners potential Soviet hostages. On 24th June 1948 the Russians were demanding a ransom.

"It's not entirely clear what the Kremlin's plans and hopes had been in the three years since the end of the war. There were those in the Soviet regime who thought in terms of a Marxist duty to world revolution—they wanted to take over western Europe just as they tucked the states of eastern Europe behind an Iron Curtain since 1945. Every state had been bankrupted by the War, wrecked by fighting, stripped by Nazi pillage. There was endemic hunger and economic depression everywhere—and neither hope nor resource to rebuild. Stalin could exploit economic misery and political unrest through increasingly popular Communist parties.

"But by early 1948 dramatic changes were clearly on the way and Germany was the key to all of them. German coal and steel were vital to refuel west European recovery. But until now, German workers had been simply too weak from hunger to

produce them—mining couldn't get up to half the pre-war level. According to the United Nations the daily ration for a healthy active man or woman was 2,650 calories. For three years since the end of the war the western zones of occupation in Germany had struggled to provide 1,500. In the terrible winter of 1946-47 some cities only got 900 calories. German industry was at a standstill—and all Germany's neighbours depended on trade with her. There was no market in Germany: the old Reichsmark was hopelessly inflated and the only acceptable currency was cigarettes. So far, the Russians had blocked every move by the West to cure the European disease; in Germany they had vetoed any common policies, in spite of a wartime agreement that Germany would be run as a single unit. They ran their zone as a separate fiefdom and were milking it dry—money, goods, anything they could lay their hands on was being shipped out to the Soviet Union. The western powers had put up with this for a while, believing that four-Power coalition was essential to secure the peace and to rebuild Europe; they had tried to buy Soviet cooperation with concessions. But by 1948, they had lost patience and decided to go it alone.

"The British and Americans, and eventually the French, had already fused their occupation zones and were running the joint economies as best they could. They now wanted to get Germans motivated, give them something to work for. In February 1948 they proposed to a west European conference in London that Germans should draft a constitution for a temporary semi-independent West German state—a stopgap until there was agreement with the Soviet Union on a unified, autonomous Germany. In June 1947 the American Secretary of State, George Marshall, had offered huge financial assistance for rebuilding the economies of Europe. That offer had been seized by the West and turned down flat by the Soviet Union—on her own behalf and that of her satellites. To crank up the west German economy in time to make use of Marshall Aid, the West had announced the introduction of a new, sound Deutschmark—it would be brought into use in the western sectors of Berlin in June 1948.

"Currency reform was the last straw for Stalin. He'd fought every western change and proposal so far and throughout 1948 he'd been venting his rage in Berlin. There was constant Soviet interference with traffic on the road and railway from the West, delay in the mail, flickering of the electricity supply. In March 1948 the Soviet Military Governor walked out of the Allied

LEFT: LOADING AND UNLOADING VITAL GOODS WAS CONTINUOUS DURING THE OPERATION; BELOW: CITIZENS OF BERLIN ARE HEARTENED BY THE SIGHT OF ANOTHER C-47 ARRIVING WITH PRECIOUS SUPPLIES.

Control Council—that was the end of four-Power government of Germany; on 16th June the Soviet representative stumped out of the Allied Kommandatura which ran Berlin—that was the end of quadripartite administration of the city and any pretence of four-Power cooperation.

"The West had not wavered in any of its policies, so on 24th June Stalin played his biggest card: total blockade of the western sectors of Berlin. The road, the railway, the electricity supply were cut. Two and a half million lives there were now at risk. Every plan for the recovery of Europe was at stake. If the western sectors were starved out it was inevitable that the Russians would take them over. Once Berlin fell, there was no hope for west German recovery: everyone in the western zones would simply wait for the Red Army to arrive. And without German coal, steel and economic momentum there would be neither the means nor the confidence in western Europe to use Marshall Aid.

"How could the western sectors possibly survive a siege? The western garrisons in the city numbered only 12,000 men in all and there were reckoned to be up to 300,000 Soviet troops surrounding them. Could a relief army break through? The chances were that west Berliners and the western garrison would be dead before it got there—and, even worse, sending in troops could spark off a war with the Russians. And the West was in no position to fight one. According to U.S. service chiefs it would take eighteen months before they were ready for it; the British Chiefs of Staff warned that meanwhile they would be unable to prevent a Soviet advance into western Germany and that would precipitate 'complete disorganization leading to disaster'. The West had only one form of military strength—Atom bombs; but everyone believed that if they used them there would be no Europe left to rebuild.

"We now know how the Berlin blockade was broken, how western Europe was saved. But an airlift didn't seem a solution to the crisis at the time. No one dreamed that it was possible to supply a great city by air. There had been major supply operations during the war—over the Hump into China, for instance. But then, there had been time for forward planning, building up stocks, laying airstrips, ensuring command of the skies. In 1948 there were no contingency plans, no preparations. There were two airfields in Berlin—Tempelhof and Gatow. Each of them had only one runway, and that was made of PSP [pierced steel planking] which would break up under heavy landings and rip

TOP: AN EMPLOYEE BADGE FROM THE AERO ENGINE DIVISION DURING WORLD WAR TWO; ABOVE: AN AIR-LIFT ANNIVERSARY COIN; TOP RIGHT: AIRLIFT CREW BETWEEN FLIGHTS; RIGHT: BRINGING MILK FOR THE CHILDREN OF BERLIN.

the tyres of laden aircraft. Access to these landing points was along three air corridors across the Soviet Zone from the West which had been allocated by the Russians in November 1945 and with remarkably little argument, which suggests how insignificant air transport had seemed at the time. Each of the corridors was twenty miles wide. They were quite as vulnerable as the road and rail links to Berlin: they could be blocked by barrage balloons, come under fire from artillery in the Soviet Zone. Navigation was no joke, even when traffic was light—and the Americans didn't even have the BABS or Rebecca Eureka aids the RAF relied on—they had to fly by radio compass and the seat of their pants. The three corridors converged in a circle of twenty miles radius over Berlin—dangerous. Ground control facilities were primitive, certainly not capable of coping with heavy traffic, let alone in bad weather. Last, but most pressing of arguments against an airlift: there were not enough aircraft to mount one. In Germany the British had six Dakotas and were expecting two squadrons more. The Americans had 100 of the Dakota's equivalent, the C-47. Each of these aircraft could carry two and a half tons. Yet every day before the blockade the western sectors of Berlin had received 9,000 tons of supplies from the West, and a further 3,000 from the East. Service chiefs in Britain and the States all argued against sending more aircraft to Germany: they were heavily committed elsewhere; the Americans in particular wanted to save time and trouble over Berlin and put all the effort into preparing for the war likely to develop from this crisis.

"It was the politicians who insisted on air rescue for Berlin. General Lucius D. Clay, the American Military Governor in Germany, tends to get the credit for starting the airlift. He did indeed ask the U.S. Air Force on 24th June to fly in food, and the next day he called for coal. In fact, the RAF got the same orders at the same time. And Clay was merely calling for a few days of morale boosting. Thereafter, he thought the only way to raise the blockade would be to send armed convoys up the Autobahn and shoot [their way] through if they were stopped. (His opponents thought this was not a clever way to start a war.) The man who from the very beginning saw the possibilities in a full scale, prolonged operation was the British Foreign Secretary, Ernest Bevin. On 25th June he ordered planning for an all-out air effort. On 28th June he laid into two American visitors, the Under Secretary for the Army and the Director of Army Plans and

Operations. He shouted at them, wheedled, jerked a few tears and told them that the United States must put everything it had into supplying the western sectors. He said afterwards: 'I really enjoyed frightening those generals.' He then spent the next few months nagging their President, Harry Truman, for big aircraft—C-54s which could carry ten tons. Truman was more than willing, but had to frighten a lot of his own generals before he got them—it was October before a vital 100 C-54s arrived in Germany.

"Neither Bevin nor Truman believed that an airlift in itself could solve the Berlin crisis. It was the only weapon to hand for the moment. And they were taking a gamble: that the Soviet Union would just stop short of shooting down aircraft and starting a war. What they wanted the airlift to do was buy time: time to get food and fuel into the western sectors and save them from quick Soviet take-over; time to impress the Kremlin with western determination and air strength. (Significantly, Bevin got American B-29 bombers stationed in England—potential nuclear [weapon] carriers. It so happened they were not loaded, but Stalin wasn't to know that.) Given time, West Germans could draft a constitution, western Europe could polish its plans for using Marshall Aid. And then, against a background of western confidence, the allies could negotiate with the Soviet Union to get the blockade lifted without making concessions over any western plan for reconstruction.

"The airlift did eventually become that vital 'cushion of time', as someone once called it. But for many months it was what the Duke of Wellington would have called a damn close run thing. Western Berlin was used to getting 12,000 tons of food and fuel a day. Once the blockade started, the city government agreed to struggle on for a while with a bare 4,000 a day, but said they would need 5,500 once winter started and more coal was consumed. Yet it took from June to the end of September before the airlift could cope with 4,500 tons a day and it was January before it could carry 5,500. The problems were overwhelming. There was the early shortage of aircraft. Then, once C-54s arrived and the British had laid on Yorks, Hastings, Sunderlands and a pot pourri of civilian machines, there was never enough time or ground crew for servicing, never an adequate supply of spare parts for maintenance. Tempelhof and Gatow had to be upgraded for landing and unloading—that meant flying in materials and heavy building equipment; seven supply airfields had to be rebuilt in the British zone and two more expanded in the American zone.

State of the art ground control facilities had to be imported. It was all very well in the early days for keen pilots to grab an aircraft, get it loaded as fast as possible, then streak off and drop into Berlin wherever there was a gap. But once the air corridors were packed with carriers, there had to be ways to stop them bumping into each other: one way traffic, take-off in blocks from rear airfields in turn, flights and landings timed to the split second.

"The early months of the airlift had required a steep learning curve in the matter of what to fly and how. Coal was a priority—for heat, light, industry. But it was bulky and heavy—and unless it was loaded properly it upset the aircraft's trim. Coal dust got everywhere and clogged controls, so sweeping had to be rigorous. Sacks were the best packaging for it, but by October the British had lost one and a third million of them and the Americans a million more—at a cost of two shillings each. Flour was another essential—and dirty load too. Bread was baked in Berlin because 15 percent of its weight is water, more than the weight of coal which had to be flown in for the bakers. Again to save weight, meat was boned, and preferably tinned or turned into sausage to preserve it—one sausage was so disgusting that not even hungry Berliners would touch it. A civil servant came up with the very Alice-in-Wonderland idea that they could be bribed to eat it by offering a double ration. They preferred to starve. Vegetables and fruit were all dried to save bulk and weight. Old Berliners remember to this day the horror of tonsil-clotting dried potato—Pom. (West German factories could never produce more than a third of the dried potato Berlin needed. British army warehouses in Egypt were stripped of stocks, then contracts were placed with Hungary, and the stuff was sent through or round Berlin to be flown back in.) Once there was enough airlift capacity, planners had to think what else a civilized society needed to keep going: newsprint, spare parts for lorries, needles and thread, shoe leather for repairs, knitting wool, x-ray plates and medical supplies. And they had to balance priorities: send all that, or use space for steel girders, heavy plant, and cement to build a brand new power station and a third airfield at Tegel, a new mascot goat for the Welsh Fusiliers, an American camel called Clarence who distributed toys and sweets to children in hospital.

"One argument, never settled, was whether to fly goods out of as well as into Berlin. The Americans always wanted the quickest possible turnaround: unload, refuel and out. The British

insisted that keeping Berlin industry ticking over was part of the whole campaign to save the western sectors. So they took a backload: anything from grand pianos to electric light bulbs: tricky loading and very time consuming. That backload explains the airlift tonnage figures about which the British have sometimes been hang dog. Between June '48 and July '49 the Americans carried one and a half million tons; the British just less than half a million. The Americans, though, stuck to standard loads, coal and flour, predictable and quick. The British took their share of them but also awkward and dangerous cargoes like salt and liquid fuel, and they added the backload.

"Everything the joint airlift achieved would have gone for nothing if it hadn't been for the courage and endurance of the Berliners who tightened their belts. They got four hours of electricity a day—if it came on in the middle of the night, that is when they did the ironing, the mending and cooked something for next day. There was no coal for heating in the winter, but they refused Russian offers of free coal, and they chopped up furniture to burn in the grate. They were under constant political assault. Democratic politicians and their supporters were beaten up or kidnapped by Soviet-controlled police, others were dragged off in the night to be interrogated by Soviet officers, were threatened with the loss of their ration cards, had their flats measured by billeting officers and their furniture confiscated. The Town Hall, which was in the Soviet sector, was several times besieged for days on end by howling, Communist-led mobs, trying to take it over. Berliners would not surrender. They said that as long as they could hear the drone of aircraft they had hope. They turned out, sometimes a quarter of a million of them at a time to hear their great mayor, Ernst Reuter, tell them that the struggle for Berlin was 'a struggle for the freedom of the world'; they backed his call to the West not to barter the city away by compromise with the Soviet Union, to 'bring help not just with aircraft but with common lasting ideals.' Then they went home and laughed at the current Berlin joke: 'Aren't we lucky. Imagine if the British and Americans were besieging us and the Russians were running the airlift.'

"That airlift delivered the means for their survival in the end. But it took a miracle to save them over the winter: the weather. Russian victories have always depended on General Winter; this time he defeated them. There was less frost and ice in Germany than ever on record—the airlift was not frozen to the ground.

The greatest bridge 1948/49 in the world

SKYWAYS

WUNSTORF — BERLIN — WUNSTORF

ABOVE: A PLASTER SOUVENIR WALL PLATE BROUGHT BACK FROM GERMANY BY A BRITISH SERVICEMAN. THESE PLATES WERE MADE IN LOCAL GERMAN WORKSHOPS AND SOLD IN CLUBS ON THE AIRLIFT BASES.

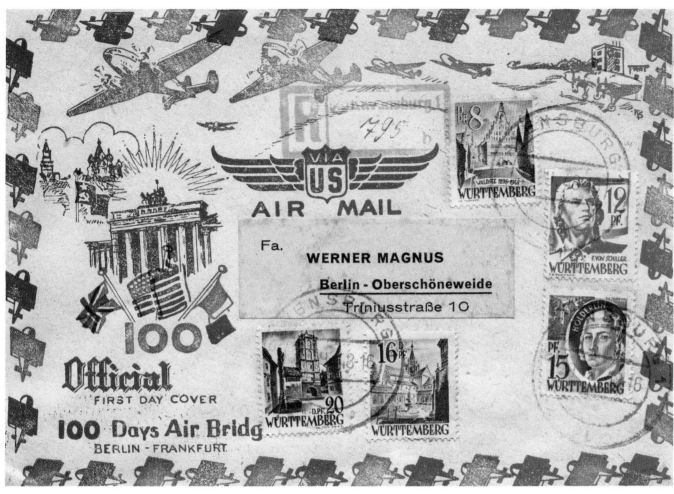

Air Vice-Marshal Cyril Siegert

CB CBE MVO DFC AFC

RAF Lyneham
Wiltshire

211

There was fog, but by then navigation and ground control could cope with it (and pilots had the skill and guts to land well under the standard safety regulations for poor visibility). And thanks to bigger and more aircraft, smooth delivery routines, nearly six and a half thousand tons a day were delivered to Berlin in March, and it was confidently predicted that the figure would soon be up to 8,000 and would keep rising. Berliners were now better fed than they had been since the war—they were actually putting on weight.

"Stalin, the realist, could read the writing on the wall. West Berlin was going to survive; thanks to the new mark and future Marshall Aid, the German economy would blossom and with it western Europe. By February 1949 German politicians in Bonn had drafted the Basic Law, a constitution for a separate west German state. That month, by no coincidence, the Soviet ambassador at the United Nations began secret talks with his American counterpart on a settlement of the Berlin crisis—and while the airlift flew and grew, there would be no need for

western concessions. The western allies had a new strength and confidence: they had agreed to set up NATO, each member would assist any other attacked. This North Atlantic Treaty was signed on 4th April; the Basic Law was approved on 9th May. And on 10th May 1949 the Russians announced they would lift the Berlin blockade.

"The airlift had been a major turning point; it had precipitated a new Europe. Sadly, it was a divided Europe: two separate and hostile political and economic systems in East and West and two armed camps, NATO and eventually the Warsaw Pact. The dividing line between them ran through Germany and split the country in two. In 1945 Germans had been seen by the occupation powers as enemies; now each German state was claimed as an ally by East and West. Divided Berlin was the potential flashpoint for any conflict between the two blocs. The western sectors were as vulnerable as ever: they still depended on food and fuel deliveries along a single road and rail link—in their anxiety to get the blockade up in May 1949, the western allies failed to negotiate better communications.

"For all its faults, this settlement for Germany and Europe turned out to be a peace settlement. It was uneasy; it gave grounds for tension and fear in the coming years, and once both sides had nuclear weapons it relied on avoidance of mutually assured destruction. Yet it gave Europe forty years of peace—the longest period in our history. And a new Europe was born in 1989 without war."

The English author/journalist George Orwell was probably the first person to use the expression "the Cold War." The 1948 Soviet blockade of Berlin was one of the first and most dangerous of many Cold War crises.

From *The Berlin Airlift* by Ann and John Tusa: "In those first two vital, chaotic weeks the British and Americans had to scour their records for men of every expertise: air-traffic controllers, mechanics, electricians, drivers, staff experienced in loading. They rummaged stores for spare parts, pierced steel planking for runways, radios, fuel lines, marshalling bats, flares, cords for lashing down freight. They rounded up lorries, jeeps, cars; signed on thousands of Germans and Displaced Persons as labourers and loaders; found stoves, pots and pans to feed the sudden influx on to the airfields.

"As if manpower, equipment and organization did not present problems enough, the airlift faced truly appalling weather. In what was supposed to be the height of summer there were thunderstorms, snow and heavy icing, fog if the wind dropped, continuous low cloud which was often below 200 feet and incessant driving rain. For three weeks and more, aircraft struggled to and from Berlin against conditions in which, as a British officer admitted, crews would not normally be asked to fly. Some American pilots encountered such icing that they had to maintain full power just to stay in the air; when they used their de-icing equipment, great lumps of ice would crack off the wings and thud down the fuselage. The RAF could seldom meet its target of 160 sorties a day because of poor visibility which prevented landings or because Gatow was closed while sheets of water were swept from the runway. Tempelhof was unusable for hours at a stretch thanks to dense cloud or violent tailwinds. Everyone on the ground was soaked to the skin—little or no protective clothing could be found. Rain seeped into the aircraft

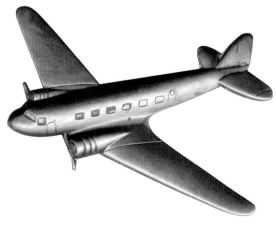

ABOVE: TWO EXAMPLES OF SOUVENIR AIRLIFT AIR CREW CIGARETTE CASES; LEFT: A BRASS C-47 DECORATIVE PIN; TOP CENTRE: A BERLIN AIRLIFT COMMEMORATIVE MEDAL; RIGHT: ADDITIONAL AIRLIFT ANNIVERSARY MAIL COVERS ISSUED IN 1998.

General Lucius D. Clay
Organisator der Luftbrücke

WUNSTORF
CELLE
FASSBERG
HAMBURG-
FUHLSBÜTTEL
LÜBECK
SCHLESWIGLAND

BERLIN
- TEGEL
- GATOW
- TEMPELHOF
- WANNSEE

FRANKFURT AM MAIN
WIESBADEN

50 JAHRE BERLINER LUFTBRÜCKE

Herrn
Karl-Jürgen Schepers
Flughafen Tegel
D - 10881 BERLIN
Deutschland / Allemagne / Germany

Zurück
Retour

BERLIN AIRLIFT

atelic Medallic Cover

08207

1948 **BERLIN AIRLIFT** 1949

Royal Mint, Llantrisant, Pontyclun CF72 8YT

RIGHT: ONE OF THE RAF DAKOTA TRANSPORTS PARTICIPATING IN THE AIRLIFT FROM GATOW AIRFIELD, BERLIN; BELOW: AIRCRAFT MAINTENANCE WAS A ROUND-THE-CLOCK JOB IN THE TIME OF THE AIRLIFT.

and engines would not start—on 2 July twenty-six Dakotas were out of service because of electrical faults caused by damp. Aircraft and motor vehicles churned the airfields into quagmires, then skidded and bogged down. Bulldozers laboured night and day to flatten the fields; PSP, rubble and bricks were thrown down to give some solid-standing. Crews waded to their aircraft through heavy, glutinous sludge, then flew in caked wellingtons or boots which glued or even froze to the rudder pedals.

"The only thing not dampened was morale. Men worked round the clock without grumbling or slacking. Pilots flew every hour the weather would let them and took frightening risks to land in minimal visibility. A Flying Control officer at Wunstorf was on duty for fourteen hours non-stop. Drivers worked for twenty-four hours without a break. Ground staff put in regular sixteen-hour shifts. High-ranking officers stood in the pouring rain and marshalled aircraft or exchanged their warm offices for a freezing aircraft packed with flour for Berlin. U.S. airmen gave up their Independence Day holiday and kept flying—the *New York Times* commented: 'We were proud of our Air Force during the war. We're prouder of it today.' Even when there was some time off, there was little rest. Aircraft and motor vehicles kept up an incessant din. American aircrews lay in rows as Nissen huts were hammered together around them and men clattered in and out, on and off duty at all hours; RAF pilots climbed ladders into attics at Wunstorf to sleep on the floor and be trampled on by people looking for a space to lie down. Other ranks, American and British, settled into sodden tents and tried to rest on the soggy ground. Everyone kept going on adrenalin. Old hands recognized 'a flap' and responded to it as they had in the war; young recruits were excited and keen to show how good they were. On paper the odds against the airlift being able to feed Berlin were impossible; the results of the first few weeks were paltry. The people involved saw only a challenge and leapt at it. Never mind the problems: 'Do your best,' 'Every little pound helps.' Men who only three years before would have set out to bomb Berlin were now using all their skill and energy to feed it. It was a target into which they put their hearts.

"And by the second week in July the airlift began to show signs of coming to grips with its problems, even though they were far from solved. Systems for handling freight had been developed, staffs of all kinds expanded, air-traffic control improved, equipment scrounged or indented for. The C-54s and

Yorks were being integrated into the operation. On 4th July half-a-dozen Sunderland flying boats landed at Finkenwerde on the Elbe and next day made their first trips to the Havel. The Russians protested at their use of the lake and claimed to control all Berlin waterways (and they were right), but they were ignored. Sunderlands could carry 10,000 lbs in their lower decks and bomb compartments. Their primary use would be to transport salt—they were anodized against salt water and their controls were tucked up out of reach of cargo so that, unlike other aircraft, they would not be corroded. They soon settled to taking other freight as well: meat, cigarettes, sanitary towels. The Havel made a natural flying boat base: calm, thanks to the shelter of low hills on all sides, with a long take-off run (often afflicted with crosswinds) and deep moorings close to the shore. Finkenwerde, on the other hand, was not ideal. The Elbe was choppy and strewn with wrecks and rubble. There were no facilities for refuelling, and the job had to be done by hand from 40-gallon drums until REME mechanics brought out a barge with a pipeline floating on jerrycans. Objectively the Sunderland itself was something of a liability—slow and ponderous, it presented scheduling problems because its run had to be slotted between those for Gatow and Tempelhof. Yet it did much to cheer the Germans, who saw it as a sign that efforts were being made and that resources were available. The ten daily Sunderland landings on the Havel attracted crowds of delighted spectators, and children especially were enchanted by this new monster duck.

"With more and bigger aircraft and better back-up, allied tonnage figures started to rise. On 8th July 1,117 tons were flown into Berlin; next day the total dropped to 819; but on 11th July it was 1,264 and by 15th July 1,480. Obviously this was still short of the 2,000 tons of food needed every day, let alone the 12,000 tons of goods in all. Even so, measured against the 1,404 tons brought in during the whole of June, it was quite an achievement.

"As the airlift grew, so did ambitions. The allies were no longer satisfied with just trying to feed Berlin. At the beginning of July Yorks carried 100 emergency generators. Pilots watched with horror as two of these 6,000-lb machines were swung into their holds without the slightest regard for the standard load factor or the usual rules for distribution of weight, and they wondered if they would get off the ground without the cargo dropping through the floor. The Americans and British flew in

kfurter Ne

petrol—a dangerous, volatile consignment which had to be carried in heavy metal drums taking up valuable space and difficult to load and secure. The backlog of letters and parcels from Berlin was cleared and more industrial goods were brought out, though the British drew the line at transporting an upright piano and a baby grand destined for export to South Africa.

"Most dramatically, the decision was taken early in July to fly in coal. The Americans had practised in their zone dropping it from the bomb bays of B-29s, but faced at the receiving end with piles of dust they soon gave up the scheme. The first coal landed at Tempelhof on 7th July packed in old service duffel bags. Nobody, two weeks before, had dreamed of bringing fuel to Berlin. Even now no one imagined that they could ever meet minimal needs. Nevertheless, coal was a new demonstration to the Russians of allied determination and capability, a new offer of hope to Berliners, another way of giving time to the politicians and diplomats to get the blockade lifted."

The foundation aircraft for the Berlin Airlift was the Douglas C-47, and the primary aircraft used at the start of the operation. In the morning of June 24th, Operation Knicker began with six RAF Dakotas carrying a daily total of sixty tons of urgently needed food and supplies between the Wunstorf base in Hanover and RAF Gatow in the British sector of Berlin. Knicker was intended as a temporary measure while the Russians were supposedly "making repairs" to the railway line used by the allies into Berlin. Three weeks later Knicker became Operation Plainfare.

At the time, General Curtis E. LeMay, a high-achieving wartime commander in the American air force, was Commander of United States Air Forces in Europe. In the early days of the airlift into Berlin, the American part of the effort was referred to as "The LeMay Coal and Feed Delivery Service." Their part was actually called Operation Vittles. The first flights in Operation Plainfare were thirty-two Dakota sorties flown on June 26th 1948. The planes delivered eighty tons of powdered milk, flour

and medicine that day. General LeMay had 102 war-weary C-47s at his disposal for most of the airlift operation and, until the arrival of 100 of the larger C-54s in October, they carried the load for the Americans. Veteran pilots and crews were grabbed from their peacetime situations in the United States, Britain and elsewhere and brought to Germany to fly the lift. As the operation grew in scope, responsibility for the American role in it passed from the U.S. Air Force to the Military Air Transport Command and a new MATC director was appointed in July. Major General William H. Tunner, the veteran commander of the wartime India to China "Hump" airlift operation, arrived in Germany to bring a higher level of efficiency to the effort. His methods earned him the nickname "Willie the Whip" when he established a system in which an aircraft was to land every three minutes, day or night, as long as the minimum ceiling at the destination was 400 feet, or better. The record for cargo tonnage delivered during the airlift was set on Sunday, April 17th 1949 when 13,000 tons were flown into Berlin. The procession of aircraft that day was referred to as the "Easter Parade."

If the winter fog, ice, clouds and rain were not bad enough to hamper the flight operations, the Soviets provided further distraction, danger, and harassment when their anti-aircraft batteries and fighter pilots fired on the American and British cargo planes. In darkness, Soviet searchlight crews did their best to wreck the night vision of the airlift pilots. All of these tactics were relatively ineffective and, in the early spring of 1949, the Russians began conversations in New York about a settlement of the Berlin situation. The resulting agreement was signed in May and the Soviet blockade was lifted. The British and Americans, however, continued to bring and stockpile great reserves of supplies, food and fuel into September against the possibility of the Soviets starting another blockade.

With the increasing availability of the larger Douglas C-54 Skymaster by October 1st, the U.S. C-47 Skytrain transports were withdrawn from primary service in the airlift. The RAF, however, continued to fly its Dakotas into Gatow and into the new airfield, Tegel, in the French zone. In fact, by November, twenty-five additional Dakota crews had arrived from the air forces of Australia, New Zealand and South Africa to supplement the RAF Dakota force and continue its contribution to the success of Plainfare. Several additional civil Dakotas were operated by half a dozen charter companies to increase the total air lift-

ing capacity in the second half of 1948.

In the fifteen months of the great airlift to Berlin, the allies delivered in excess of 2.3 million tons of vitally needed cargo. There were crashes and fatalities. Thirty military personnel and one civilian died in the operation.

SUPPLIES DELIVERED IN THE BERLIN AIRLIFT IN U.S. TONS

U.S.

FLIGHTS	189,963
TOTAL	1,783,572
FOOD	296,319
COAL	1,421,118
OTHER	66,134
PASSENGERS IN	25,263
PASSENGERS OUT	37,486

BRITISH

FLIGHTS	87,841
TOTAL	541,936
FOOD	240,386
COAL	164,910
OTHER	136,640
PASSENGERS IN	34,815
PASSENGERS OUT	130,091

FRENCH

FLIGHTS	424
TOTAL	800
FOOD	UNKNOWN
COAL	UNKNOWN
OTHER	UNKNOWN
PASSENGERS IN | OUT	10,000

TOTAL U.S., BRITISH AND FRENCH

FLIGHTS	278,228
TOTAL	2,325,509
FOOD	536,705
COAL	1,586,029
OTHER	202,775
PASSENGERS IN	UNKNOWN
PASSENGERS OUT	UNKNOWN

ON FILM

IN THIS SECTION THE
MOTION PICTURE AND TELE-
VISION IMAGES ARE SHOWN
IN STILLS FROM SEVERAL
FILMS THAT HAVE FEATURED
DC-2S, DC-3S, AND C-47S,
FROM 1934 TO 2001. THE
FILM TITLES ARE LISTED
CHRONOLOGICALLY.

LEFT: IN THE 1956 RKO
THRILLER *BACK FROM
ETERNITY*, GENE BARRY AND
PHYLLIS KIRK STAR ALONG
WITH ANITA EKBERG, ROD
STEIGER, AND ROBERT RYAN.
WHEN A DC-3 CRASH-LANDS
IN HEADHUNTER COUNTRY,
ONLY FIVE OF THE EIGHT
PASSENGERS WILL SURVIVE.

BRIGHT EYES (FOX, 1934)
LOST HORIZON (COLUMBIA, 1937)
FLIGHT INTO NOWHERE (COLUMBIA, 1938)
TEST PILOT (MGM, 1938)
SKY GIANT (RKO, 1938)
STUNT PILOT (MONOGRAM, 1939)
TOPPER TAKES A TRIP (UNITED ARTISTS, 1939)
NICK CARTER MASTER DETECTIVE (MGM, 1939)
MY FAVORITE WIFE (RKO, 1940)
FLIGHT ANGELS (WARNER BROTHERS, 1940)
SKY MURDER (MGM, 1940)
FLYING BLIND (PARAMOUNT, 1941)
WHISTLING IN THE DARK (MGM, 1941)
FORCED LANDING (PARAMOUNT, 1941)
KEEP 'EM FLYING (UNIVERSAL, 1941)
THE BRIDE CAME C.O.D. (WARNER BROTHERS, 1941)
WOMAN OF THE YEAR (MGM, 1942)
BERLIN CORRESPONDENT (FOX, 1942)
SHERLOCK HOLMES IN WASHINGTON (UNIVERSAL, 1943)
LADIES COURAGEOUS (UNIVERSAL, 1943)
A GUY NAMED JOE (MGM, 1943)
WE'VE NEVER BEEN LICKED (UNIVERSAL, 1943)
THIRTY SECONDS OVER TOKYO (MGM, 1944)
OBJECTIVE BURMA (WARNER BROTHERS, 1945)
GOD IS MY CO-PILOT (WARNER BROTHERS, 1945)
THEY WERE EXPENDABLE (MGM, 1945)
CORNERED (RKO, 1945)
YOU CAME ALONG (PARAMOUNT, 1945)
NOTORIOUS (RKO, 1946)
THE BEGINNING OF THE END (MGM, 1946)
BUCK PRIVATES COME HOME (UNIVERSAL, 1947)
BLAZE OF NOON (PARAMOUNT, 1947)
YOU GOTTA STAY HAPPY (UNIVERSAL, 1948)
COMMAND DECISION (MGM, 1948)
ILLEGAL ENTRY (UNIVERSAL, 1949)
FRANCIS (UNIVERSAL, 1949)

RIGHT: THE UNITED ARTISTS PRODUCTION OF *A BRIDGE TOO FAR* TELLS THE STORY OF THE 1944 ALLIED DEFEAT AT ARNHEM IN HOLLAND. THE PARATROOPER AND GLIDER LANDINGS IN THE ACTUAL BATTLE, OPERATION MARKET-GARDEN, EMPLOYED HUNDREDS OF C-47S. THE FILM WAS BASED ON THE BOOK BY CORNELIUS RYAN AND STARRED RYAN O'NEAL, RIGHT, AS GENERAL JAMES GAVIN, JAMES CAAN, EDWARD FOX, MICHAEL CAINE, SEAN CONNERY, LIV ULLMAN, LAURENCE OLIVIER, ROBERT REDFORD, GENE HACKMAN, ARTHUR HILL, DIRK BOGARDE, AND MAXIMILIAN SCHELL.

LEFT: *FLIGHT INTO NOWHERE* WAS A 1938 COLUMBIA PICTURE THAT FEATURED JACK HOLT AND WARD BOND.

THE BIG LIFT (FOX, 1950)
THE THING (RKO, 1951)
AIR CADET (UNIVERSAL, 1951)
THE LOST CONTINENT
(LIPPERT, 1951)
CALLING BULLDOG DRUM-
MOND (MGM, 1951)
JUNGLE JIM (SERIES,
COLUMBIA, 1952)
BIG JIM MCLAIN (U.S., 1952)
RETREAT HELL! (WARNER
BROTHERS, 1952)
FLIGHT NURSE (U.S., 1953)
ISLAND IN THE SKY
(WARNER BROTHERS, 1953)
BEAST FROM 20,000 FATH-
OMS (WARNER BROTHERS,
1953)
EAST OF SUMATRA
(UNIVERSAL, 1953)
THE HIGH AND THE MIGHTY
(WARNER BROTHERS, 1954)
STRATEGIC AIR COMMAND
(PARAMOUNT, 1955)
THE ETERNAL SEA
(REPUBLIC, 1955)
THE SEA CHASE (WARNER
BROTHERS, 1955)
THIS ISLAND EARTH
(UNIVERSAL, 1955)
TOP OF THE WORLD (UNITED
ARTISTS, 1955)
BACK FROM ETERNITY (RKO,
1956)
JET PILOT (U.S., 1957)
THE DEADLY MANTIS (U.S.,
1957)
CHINA DOLL (U.S.A.F., 1958)
NEVER SO FEW (MGM, 1959)
PARATROOP COMMAND
(AMERICAN INTERNATIONAL,
1959)
THE GALLANT HOURS
(UNITED ARTISTS, 1960)
BACK STREET (UNIVERSAL,
1961)
FLIGHT FROM ASHIYA (U.S.,
1963)
IN HARM'S WAY
(PARAMOUNT, 1965)
MCHALE'S NAVY JOINS THE
AIR FORCE (UNIVERSAL,
1965)
NONE BUT THE BRAVE
(WARNER BROTHERS, 1965)
CAST A GIANT SHADOW
(UNITED ARTISTS, 1966)
THE DIRTY DOZEN (MGM,
1967)
TERROR IN THE JUNGLE
(CROWN INTERNATIONAL,
1967)
THE HELL WITH HEROES
(UNIVERSAL 1968)

RIGHT: IN 1952, ALAN LADD, (THIRD FROM LEFT), STARRED IN *THE BIG JUMP*, AKA *THE RED BERET*, AKA *THE PARATROOPER*, A WARWICK PRODUCTIONS, UK FILM; BELOW: WARNER BROTHERS PRODUCTION OF *NONE BUT THE BRAVE*, WITH FRANK SINATRA, CLINT WALKER AND BRAD DEXTER, A MELODRAMA ABOUT U.S. MARINES IN THE PACIFIC DURING WWII.

LEFT: *PARATROOP COMMAND*, A 1959 FILM FROM AMERICAN INTERNATIONAL WITH JACK HOGAN, RICHARD BAKALYAN AND CAROLYN HUGHES; BELOW: THE UNITED ARTISTS' 1977 FILM *THE EAGLE HAS LANDED*, FROM THE JACK HIGGINS NOVEL, WITH MICHAEL CAINE, DONALD SUTHERLAND, ROBERT DUVALL AND JENNY AGUTTER.

GREEN BERETS (WARNER BROTHERS, 1968)
TOPAZ (U.S., 1969)
SKULLDUGGERY (UNIVERSAL, 1970)
PATTON (FOX, 1970)
LOST HORIZON (UNIVERSAL, 1973)
LIVE AND LET DIE (UNITED ARTISTS, 1973)
DAKOTA (DUTCH, 1974)
THE EAGLE HAS LANDED (UNITED ARTISTS 1977)
A BRIDGE TOO FAR (UNITED ARTISTS, 1977)
THE WILD GEESE (UNITED ARTISTS, 1978)
THE ISLAND (UNIVERSAL, 1980)
THE RIGHT STUFF (WARNER BROTHERS, 1983)
LONE WOLF MCQUADE (U.S., 1983)
ROCKY IV (MGM, 1985)
VOLUNTEERS (U.S., 1985)
CLUB PARADISE (U.S., 1986)
HOT PURSUIT (PARAMOUNT, 1987)
SKY PIRATES (AUSTRALIAN, 1987)
GORILLAS IN THE MIST (UIP/WARNER, 1988)
MAJOR LEAGUE (MIRAGE, 1989)
INDIANA JONES AND THE LAST CRUSADE (PARAMOUNT, 1989)
HOW I GOT INTO COLLEGE (U.S., 1989)
AIR AMERICA (TRI STAR, 1990)
DANGER ISLAND (TV, 1992)
DIEN BIEN PHU (FRENCH, 1992)
THE COVER GIRL MURDERS (TV, 1993)
DROP ZONE (PARAMOUNT, 1994)
TERMINAL VELOCITY (HOLLYWOOD PICTURES, 1994)
RICHIE RICH (WARNER BROTHERS, 1994)
OUTBREAK (WARNER BROTHERS, 1995)
CONGO (UIP/ PARAMOUNT, 1995)
RANSOM (BUENA VISTA/ TOUCHSTONE, 1996)
BRIDGE OF TIME (TV, 1997)
THE THIN RED LINE (FOX, 1998)
BAND OF BROTHERS (TV, 2001)

LEFT: *FLYING BLIND*, WITH
RICHARD ARLEN AND JEAN
PARKER, PARAMOUNT, 1941;
ABOVE: RONALD COLEMAN IN
LOST HORIZON, WITH JANE
WYATT, THOMAS MITCHELL
AND SAM JAFFE.

RIGHT: ALL-TIME LITTLE CHARMER SHIRLEY TEMPLE IN THE 1934 FOX FILM *BRIGHT EYES*, WITH JAMES DUNN, LOIS WILSON AND JANE WITHERS. THE FILM FEATURED SCENES IN A DC-2 AIRLINER.

Andrew Davenport flies the C-47 N1944A for shipping executive Peter Livanos: "I started flying when I was fourteen, in the A.T.C., flying gliders and Chipmunks. I had always wanted to be a pilot but I was in my mid-twenties before I finally learned to fly. Eventually, I went on to become a flying instructor and then an air taxi pilot, survey pilot, and ferry pilot. I started off flying a Hawker 125 based in the UK, and went, from there, on to the Gulfstream III, IV, and 550, so my background has been in civil flying. Nearly all my commercial flying has been corporate. My connection to this aircraft [the C-47, N1944A] came about because I was flying Gulfstreams for its owner and the opportunity arose in 2005 to get involved with the C-47. It was a big step for me. When I went and looked at it, I thought, 'Do I really want to do this? It's quite an intimidating aeroplane at first sight, and despite flying bigger and heavier aeroplanes, this looked quite a handful. It was also a big responsibility because of its heritage'. So, I had to think long and hard before I decided I'd take up the challenge.

"I am currently flying the Gulfstream 550 for Mr Livanos and twice a year I go out to Savannah, Georgia, for recurrent training on type. Of his other aeroplanes, I currently fly the Stearman. I've got some time on a Harvard, but as yet I haven't flown the Livanos Harvard. When it is relocated to Oxford, I'll get checked out and, eventually, I hope to go on and fly the Spitfire. We'll see how it goes. Again, that's a big responsibility, so I do take it very seriously.

"I have about ninety hours on the Dakota [N1944A], coming into my third year of flying it. During the war, I think that the Airspeed Oxford and/or the Anson were used as transition aircraft onto the Dakota. I suppose the Americans might have used the Beech 18 to fulfill the same role.

"With regard to the handling qualities of the Dak, I find it very heavy in all its axies. Once it's away from the ground, it's a delight to fly even though it's heavy. Close to the ground, it's a little bit more challenging, especially on landing and particularly if there is a crosswind. But that's the same for most tailwheel aeroplanes. Although the aircraft has got a lot of inertia, it takes a lot of rudder and a lot of aileron to keep directional control. Obviously, like many old twin-engined aeroplanes, on one engine it is a handful. If you were to lose an engine on take-off, the priority is to get the gear up, followed closely by feathering the prop on the failed side, because it simply will not climb. On a single-engine approach, you don't want to attempt a go-around below 500 feet AGL when fully configured to land. The reason being that, in order to maintain speed in the go-around, you are going to descend while you are cleaning up the aeroplane.

"I suppose that one of the Dak's most endearing qualities is that it is not particularly easy to fly well—just like a Tiger Moth—but if you can fly it well, it is very satisfying. However, this satisfaction is always tempered by the sense of responsibility. You can't replace the aeroplane; you can't replace its history. There were about ten and a half thousand DC-3s built, maybe 100 pilots for each aircraft. Let's say that one million pilots world-wide have flown DC-3s, and it seems that there are probably a million different ways to fly a DC-3. Everybody's got their own ideas, and the more people you talk to, the more things you learn about operating the aeroplane. What we are trying to achieve here in our operation, is to go through everything—all the different techniques, all the engineering points of the aeroplane—and to find the best way to operate it, learning from more experienced people around the world. Unfortunately, our experience pool is drying up because there are fewer and fewer operators. I think that there are currently seven DC-3s flying in the UK now. It's probably easier to find a current and qualified Spitfire pilot here in the UK than it is to find a suitably qualified DC-3 pilot. We currently have four pilots in our operation: John Dodd, Bill Tollett, Clive Edwards, and myself.

"We fly it by day VMC only. We try to avoid cloud and bad weather as we don't want to get wet in the cockpit! As we are not flying day-in, day-out, I think that's a prudent way to approach the operation of the aeroplane. Yes, you get hydraulic fluid and oil on you, but you'll never go rusty flying this aeroplane.

"When I did my initial training on the DC-3, the instructor was extremely nervous about stalling it; he didn't want to stall it. We had to simulate a stall. However, when I went back for my recurrent training, we stalled it clean and we stalled it in 20 degree banked turns with gear and flaps down. It does give you plenty of warning. There is quite a positive pre-stall buffet and so when it did stall, it wasn't a surprise.

"I had an engine failure while training on my fourth take-off in the aeroplane. We had just briefed that we were going to carry out a practice engine failure, and we had a partial failure for real. It took me a little while to convince the instructor that I was not over-acting. We had lost power on the right engine just after take-off. That was at Chino in California. As a result, every time I take off, I mentally prepare myself for an engine failure. Planning for the worst and hoping for the best, if you like. Obviously, the most risky [such incident] is an engine failure on take-off, particularly if the aircraft is heavy.

"On a day when we are going to fly the aeroplane, the first thing we look at is the weather. It's the first priority for all aviators. We've got very strict criteria for how we operate. We try to pick our route where the weather is going to be best and, if we are going to land somewhere, where the winds favour the runways we are going to be using. Our engineer arrives an hour or two before I get here, to pre-oil both engines. Warm oil is hand-pumped around each engine and that takes about an hour for both. We carefully pull the engines through fifteen blades to ensure that we don't have a hydraulic lock, which is when oil pools in one or more of the lower cylinders. Ideally, this is performed by a minimum of two people. Both pilots and an engineer generally make a walk-around [inspection], including checking fuel and oil quantities for each engine. As the fuel gauges are inaccurate—I don't know of any DC-3s with accurate fuel gauges—we use a dipstick to measure quantities in the four fuel tanks in the wings. To move the aeroplane out of the hangar using a tug and strops attached to the undercarriage, we have someone in the cockpit guarding the brakes, someone at each wing, and someone on the tail to steer the aircraft using its tow bar. Once it is outside, we ensure that we have somebody in the cockpit before any control locks are removed, particularly the rudder lock. The rudder has a large area and can be slammed against its stops in surprisingly light winds, causing damage. We generally leave the gear pins in for engine start with an engineer in attendance. We start [the engines] with either fire crew, or an engineer, in attendance with a fire extinguisher. I've seen some spectacular photographs following a 'wet start' with flames all

RIGHT: OF THE MANY FINE EXAMPLES OF AIRCRAFT AND AVIATION-RELATED PROMOTIONAL ITEMS, THIS LARGE CIGAR BOX LABEL IS PARTICULARLY PLEASING; PRECEDING SPREAD: THE C-47 OF THE BATTLE OF BRITAIN MEMORIAL FLIGHT.

SAN TELMO CIGAR CO.,INC.

Airliner

BAY CITY, MICHIGAN.

around the outside of the engine nacelle.

"We normally start the No 2 (right) engine first. Our technique is that the pilot sitting in the left seat will start the No 2 engine, and the pilot in the right seat can keep an eye on what's going on. It's quite a juggling procedure to get the engines started. We've got a very basic energizer-mesh system: two switches on the overhead panel. As soon as the pilot observing sees the propeller rotation, he calls it. The fuel pump is turned on and we start priming. This is for a cold start. We count fifteen blades and then turn on the right magneto, bring the mixture up and keep priming as necessary. Hopefully, it will start as it invariably does when it's cold. When it is warm, it requires a different technique. Then it is very easy to flood and, consequently, presents an increased fire risk.

"When we have the No 2 engine started, we run the appropriate checklists, checking different hydraulic systems, and then the pilot in the right seat will start the No 1 (left) engine, with the pilot in the left seat observing. We hand the control of the aircraft from one pilot to the other and then it comes back again. Somebody has always got the checklist; somebody is always watching the engines. A warm start may require only six blades and no priming. Just turn the magnetos on and it might start; you might have to tickle the primer and then bring the mixture up very slowly. Each engine is different. They've got their own personalities, in a way. But that's nice. Part of the aeroplane's character.

"Once the engines are running, we need the cylinder head temperatures to be up to a minimum of 120, oil temperature up to 40 celsius. We let the engines warm up slowly. Depending on the ambient temperature of the day, you could be sitting there for ten to fifteen minutes waiting for the T's and P's to come up. What we don't want to do is give the engine any temperature shocks by increasing power before it is ready to go.

"Visibility in the three-point attitude isn't brilliant, but that's the same with all tailwheel aeroplanes. Your eyeline is about fourteen feet above the ground.

"For the take-off, we make sure the tailwheel lock is engaged because directional control is going to be a nightmare if it's not. As the control yoke rotates through 180 degrees, with a crosswind take-off you find that you are flying the initial part of the take-off with your arms crossed. You then have to uncross them and feed it round as you are accelerating. The sooner you get the tail in the air, the better, because you've then got improved directional control provided by the rudder. We're looking for eighty-four knots. If we

RIGHT AND BELOW: PILOT ANDREW DAVENPORT FLIES THE C-47 N1944A FOR WINGS VENTURE. HE IS SHOWN INSPECTING THE PLANE AT KIDLINGTON, ENGLAND. HE ALSO FLIES THE OWNER'S GULFSTREAM BUSINESS JET.

have a serious problem prior to eighty-four knots, we would abort and try to stop the aeroplane on the runway. The other options, if we are not able to stop on the runway, are either to retract the landing gear, or groundloop the aeroplane. Consequently, we aim to use a minimum runway length of 1,000 metres. The aeroplane is much more capable than that, but it gives us an added safety margin should anything go wrong. At eighty-four knots we take the aeroplane into the air and the priority then is to get the gear up and get away from the ground. Should you have an engine failure, you need to 'hurry up, slowly'. It is then a joint decision by the two pilots to identify the failed engine before we do anything about feathering a propeller.

"We're looking for a safety speed of ninety-one knots to fly the aeroplane on one engine with the gear up and one propeller feathered, so that's our initial target speed just after take-off. As we pass through 105 knots we start bringing the power back during the climb. If you've got a long runway—somewhere like Fairford—there is no rush to get the gear up because if you do have an engine problem, it's far better to just put the aircraft back on the runway. Each take-off is different in that respect. It's not automatic to get the gear up immediately. At somewhere like Oxford [airport], which has only got about 5,000 feet, if we get the aeroplane into the air, there is little chance that we could get it down again and stopped before going off the end of the runway, so we are better off taking it into the air on one engine, bringing it round and coming back. But that's just basic airmanship and not specific to the DC-3.

"We tend to stay fairly low—1,500 feet—which gives people a chance to see and hear the aeroplane. It's also more fun for us. When you look out of the cockpit window at its shadow sliding over the ground, it's fantastic. We haven't got much in the way of avionics on the aeroplane, although we do have a portable GPS as a back-up. With the amount of controlled air space around the UK, you can't afford to infringe, especially with such a high-profile aircraft. I read somewhere that, if you do have an uncontrolled engine fire, you may lose the wing in about a minute, so being at 1,500 feet gives you a chance. If we were unfortunate enough to find ourselves in that position, we could get the aeroplane on the ground somewhere—in a field if necessary, in short order.

"To get set up to land, I start quite a few miles out. There are different techniques for working out your rate of descent. From 1,500 feet you really don't have to worry about that. I try to bring back the manifold pressure—say, we're at about thirty inches of manifold

pressure at 2,050 rpm—that's about the cruise that we normally use at low level. The mixture would be in auto-lean. What I try to do some way out is to start bringing the manifold pressure back about an inch per minute, so that we arrive near the aerodrome with about twenty-five inches of manifold pressure at 2,050 rpm. Continuing to reduce the manifold pressure as we come round into the circuit, I get the aeroplane slowed down. The maximum speed for [lowering] the landing gear is 140 knots and I'm looking to get the gear down fairly early. As soon as we are established downwind, I call for quarter flap and the mixture will be returned to auto-rich, helping to keep the engines cool. I gradually reduce the manifold pressure to get below ninety-nine knots, followed by half flap. Ninety-seven knots and three-quarter flap before turning on to base leg. Then, depending on what the wind is doing and how far we are from the runway, full flap. We are aiming for about eighty-five knots on final approach and seventy-five knots at the threshold.

"As we approach the runway threshold, I start to reduce the power until it's at idle. Then, I start to pull back on the yoke to flare the aeroplane and, at the same time, push the propeller levers to fine, in case we have to make a go-around. Then, just hold the aeroplane off until the wheels touch. As soon as they touch, I push forward to keep the tail in the air and main wheels on the runway. I don't three-point the aeroplane. It *can* be three-pointed, but the short-field technique is to roll the aeroplane on. With the tail in the air, you do have a little bit more directional control with the rudder.

"If you've got a crosswind during the landing rollout, you may have the yoke rotated for maximum deflection, especially in strong crosswinds. This particular aeroplane has the old expander-type brakes—its original wartime brakes, which are pretty inefficient. I can actually use the brakes with the tail in the air. So, I balance the pitching moment created by the brakes, with the elevator. Some of the later DC-3/C-47 aircraft have been retrofitted with more efficient disc brakes, so the brake pedals can't be touched with the tail in the air because of the risk of pitching over on to its nose. While I've still got the tail in the air it is relatively easy to keep the aeroplane straight with a bit of brake if needed. Once the tail is on the ground, the aeroplane becomes slightly more demanding as I have now lost a lot of rudder authority. I might need a dab of brake, a touch of asymetric power, to keep the plane straight in the crosswind. Then, hopefully, I can taxi off the runway and breathe a sigh of relief.

"After blocking in following a flight, we just let everything settle down for a minute or so before we shut the engines down. I don't know how the airlines did it. I suspect they weren't as diligent. I don't know, but I can't see how they could run a proper scheduled service, taking as much time as we do to do things. But it's a different world now.

"There have been a few memorable occasions over the last couple of years. My very first flight I made on this particular aeroplane was out of Kemble. We got airborne, went off for a twenty or thirty minute local flight, came back and we had a flap problem. The flaps would only partially extend and I ended up too high to make the landing, so I had to go around. We came back again and the wind had changed, so they changed the runway on us. I had to go around for a second time. We made the landing at the third attempt, but I thought that it was a little too exciting for my very first flight on the aeroplane. It turned out that the pressure relief valve on the flap circuit had been calibrated incorrectly. The air loads were too high for the flaps to extend. Another highlight was to take the aircraft back to Upottery, its D-Day base, in August of 2007. The airfield has been disused since 1945 and it was special to be taking it back for the first time since 1944."

Fergus Mayhew currently flies a Gulfstream 550 for Tag Aviation. He has logged approximately 550 hours flying the Douglas DC-3: "I first flew the aircraft in the summer of 1986, for Provincetown-Boston Airlines who flew, in the summer, from Cape Cod to Boston and to the islands of Martha's Vineyard and Nantucket. In the winter, the whole fleet moved south and they flew from Miami down to Key West and to the west resorts in Florida.

"That was my first commercial airline job. I had flown helicopters in the North Sea and a Jet Ranger for a Yorkshireman. A commuter airline is like a stepping stone to the major airlines; most people stayed there three or four years and then moved on to the airlines. The pay was poor—fifteen thousand dollars a year for a first officer and about twenty-five thousand a year for a captain, which, even in the mid-'80s, wasn't that good. But you'd only stay there a few years and then you'd usually get a right seat with a major airline. From Provincetown-Boston Airlines I went to work for Hunting Cargo Airlines, flying a Merchantman, which is the biggest Vanguard. After Hunting, I went to Danair and flew 727s and then went back to Hunting, and then to Easyjet. I had been with Hunting for a total of eight years, two years with Danair and five with Easyjet.

"The DC-3 was such a huge leap forward in aircraft design in 1935. It was really the first proper airliner and it was a pleasure to fly. It was a very safe aircraft. The passengers enjoyed it. The radial engines were nice. The look and feel, the vibration—everything about the aircraft was nice and gentle, but it could also be a bit of a handful, which made it a challenge as well. It wasn't completely docile; it could bite back at you and you always had to be on your guard. Being a tail-wheel aircraft made it a lot more demanding. If it had been designed as a nose-wheel aircraft, I think it would have been much less exceptional, and being a tail-wheel aircraft actually made it a lot more fuel-efficient. You could land it on very short strips. And as Eisenhower said, it was one of the key machines that won the war.

"Provincetown-Boston Airlines had the first [DC-3] aircraft to reach 100,000 hours on the airframe, which was PB-36, and is now with the Smithsonian. That particular aircraft was delivered to Eddie Rickenbacker, who founded Eastern Airlines, and I was flying it because my company, PBA, was taken over by Continental and Eastern Airlines in 1986, becoming Eastern Express. Rickenbacker took delivery of it new in 1936; fifty years later I was back flying it for Eastern again.

"Once the aircraft was in the air, it was extremely pleasant to fly and very easy to fly on instruments. You could do a perfect instrument landing system approach; it was very good for EVRs and non-directional beacons. When the aircraft was on the ground, and you had the wind down the runway, no problem. But, if you had a strong crosswind, the aircraft required some quite advanced technique to take off. Basically, to get full aileron deflection, you had to travel the yoke through 270 degrees and often you had to use differential thrust to keep the aeroplane straight on the runway. Landing was interesting in gusting crosswinds as well. In ordinary flying, it wasn't much of a problem.

"The aircraft was very capable, fully IFR-capable, but we did have this one problem at Boston Logan—a very busy airport. We had jets coming up behind us and we had to make an approach at 140 knots and then slow down to ninety-five knots to put the flaps out, and of course, we couldn't do this until the last minute which, visually, wasn't a problem. But if we were on an ILS it was a big problem—we'd have to climb to get our speed off to get the flaps out. So, what would happen is we'd bring the power back to fifteen inches of manifold pressure and then we would climb at about a thousand feet per minute and get the speed back to ninety-five knots, pop the flaps out and then nose the aircraft over and recapture the glide slope. Officially, this was totally illegal because if you go more than one dot glide slope deflection you're supposed to go around, and of course, we weren't one dot, we were lying complete full-scale glide slope deflection at the outer marker inbound at 1,200 or 1,300 feet. But, it was the only way to operate the aircraft into Logan, so our chief pilot just looked the other way, and that's how we did it. The DC-3 was probably the worst offender because it had such a slow final approach speed. It's flaps were called split flaps and were very flimsy and that's why it was only ninety-five knots.

"The engines were absolutely fantastic—very forgiving. On a wet, cold morning they could often be quite difficult to start and required quite a bit of skill. It was a matter of turning them over and then knowing exactly when to put the mixture to full rich to get the engine to fire. There's a lot of tender loving care required when starting a radial engine. Generally, once you got your engines started, it was fine. Never really had any problem with the engines.

" We had some very basic instrumentation. [Our DC-3s] had different instruments in each aircraft. The radios were all in different positions because they had come from different companies. Some of them had very crude instrumentation. There was no HIS—horizontal situation indicator. You just had a drum directional indicator, which was confusing. We were expected to do Category One ILS's down to 200 feet into Provincetown, Martha's Vineyard and Nantucket, and we often did. It's very rare to actually have to go around because, usually by 200 feet, you broke out of the fog and saw the lights.

"I came from flying as a flight instructor to flying a DC-3, and I did find that it was pretty demanding to take off this aircraft. Being a very large tail-dragger, it was 30,000 pounds in max take-off weight, if I remember. It carried thirty people in some comfort. The cabin decoration was done out in a pretty interesting way. Actually, it quite often looked like Grandma's parlour. You had pictures that had been screwed into the bulkhead—really quite poor paintings of cornfields in Massachusetts, for instance. Every plane was done up differently.

"My captains all operated in different ways. Many of them,

DAVENPORT: "WE'VE PROBABLY GOT ONE OF THE BEST ENGINEERED DC-3S. WE MAINTAIN IT TO COMMERCIAL STANDARDS; TO A HIGHER DEGREE THAN IS REQUIRED BY THE AUTHORITIES."

when they landed the aircraft, insisted that you always have twenty inches of manifold pressure as you landed; others said, 'No, no, you take all the power off at 100 feet and dead-stick it on.' I found, whenever I tried that, it always got a bit nasty. We started doing some very heavy landings, so I decided that landing it with power was probably the best idea. There were no proper standard operating procedures because it was a Part 135 carrier. The FAA basically weren't that interested in controlling them in the '80s. It's different now, but in those days, as long as you didn't have a crash, the FAA left you alone.

"Unfortunately, I did have a crash in one. The H-frame, which is the rear member that keeps the landing gear extended, had fractured and was falling loose. Even more unfortunately, the air traffic control in Hyannis decided that it wasn't really worth mentioning, so, when we landed, the left undercarriage folded up into the undercarriage bay and the left propeller then bit into the runway, which made the aircraft go on its nose. Then the right prop bit into the runway and we stayed on our nose. The captain, Mitch McNabb, who was from Alabama, said: 'Well, hell, Fergus, I think you should close down here and I'll go back and see how our passengers are.' So, rather shaken, I hurriedly closed down all fuel valves and oil valves that I could

find. A DC-3 cockpit isn't very complicated so that didn't take too long. Mitch came back and said: 'Oh, we'll get everybody off now.' Of course, we did happen to have one chancer on board who said, 'Oh, my back's gone,' which annoyed all the pilots in PBA, who said: 'We'll give him some back problems.' Other than that unfortunate incident, I found the plane very safe.

"There were a few uncomfortable things. If it was raining heavily and you were in a turn, you'd often get a large dump of water straight between your legs—usually with the captain laughing because it always seemed to happen to the first officer rather than him.

"Famous people we carried included Tip O'Neill, who was the Speaker of the House of Representatives. He'd travel across from Boston to Cape Cod where he had a house and he was a regular passenger with us. He was an absolutely charming man, and so huge that he always took up two seats. We occasionally had Teddy Kennedy on board as well, going to Martha's Vineyard."

"The DC-3 was, and is, unique, for no other flying machine has been a part of the international scene and action so many years, cruised every sky known to mankind, been so ubiqui-

tous, admired, cherished, glamourized, known the touch of so many different pilot nationals, and sparked so many maudlin tributes. It was without question the most all-up successful aircraft ever built and even in this jet age it seems likely the surviving Douglas DC-3s may fly about their business forever."
— Ernest K. Gann

Skydiver Martin Evans: "It was during the Phoenix Z-Hills Easter Boogie. We were on the DC-3 *Phoenix Air* with our skydiving group, taking off for our final jump of the day. We had had a good day's skydiving and a great few weeks skydiving with old and new friends. As we left the ground our spirits were high.

"A few seconds later, at an altitude of only 350 feet, we lost an engine. We glanced at each other and I thought 'It's no big deal. A DC-3 can maintain, even climb, on one engine.' A moment later, contrary to what we believed from previous experiences to be true, this time things were different. We realized we were in a potentially catastrophic situation. It was as if time slowed down and seconds seemed to become minutes as the aircraft sank towards the earth. We each prepared for the impact in our own way. Strangely, there was no screaming or panic. But maybe that was not so strange in that most of us were conditioned to reacting in life-threatening situations. Few people ever find themselves in a truly life-threatening situation and have the time to take it all in. If ever they do, they may be as astonished as many of us were that day to find that it really isn't that scary. There is no time to be scared, not if you determine to survive.

"As those around me braced themselves for the impact, I suddenly realized that I was the only one on board who was not strapped in. This, in spite of the fact that nearly a year before, skydiving had lost many friends in the Perris Valley Otter crash. It seemed we hadn't all learned the lessons of that terrible day. I quickly hunkered down on the floor and braced myself tightly while chastising myself for being such a fool.

"I was still berating myself when we hit. I cannot be certain if there were any screams or utterances. There was the noise of the aircraft breaking up as we hurtled across the ground. Though we had descended in a long glide rather than at a steep angle, the impact was considerable. We had ripped through high tension power lines near the end of our descent. We hit the ground and crossed a slight rise, getting us airborne again for another

brief moment. We slammed down again and were bumping and grinding across the ground for what seemed an eternity. I tightened my grip and tried to prepare for the inevitable sudden stop.

"We spun off to the right and banged into something, but still were not stopping. There was another impact and those on the benches fell down on those of us on the floor. The plane bumped and ground along some more and I'm sure that most of us thought that our lives were at an end. And then the motion stopped. We all seemed to be alive and in relatively good shape.

"But we were still in the aircraft and, though there was no evidence of smoke or fire at that moment, we knew we had to get out and away from the plane before it caught fire. We got out as quickly as we could, being sure to leave no one behind. As the last person left the jump door, I glanced towards the cockpit area and saw a pair of legs dangling through the pilot's escape hatch. I re-entered the cabin and ran to the cockpit where I pulled our pilot, Herman Reinhold, out of the hatch, and ran back down the cabin and out to where the others were gathered some distance from the plane. We all expected the DC-3 to explode or erupt in flames, but it never did.

"The end result of the incident was a pilot with bruised ribs and a wrecked DC-3. Injuries suffered among the forty of us amounted to one sprained ankle and a few small abrasions. In my opinion, we owe our lives to the expertise, calm control, skill and presence of mind of the pilot.

"Seatbelts in jump planes, and all other planes, are provided for your safety and the safety of others around you. Use them. You may not be as lucky as I was in this incident if you fail to buckle up."

Henry Tyndall "Dick" Merrill was unparalleled among airmen and airline pilots. This descendant of the American hunter-trailblazer Daniel Boone, was born in Luka, Mississippi in 1894 and died in California on October 31st 1982. Like his famous ancestor, Merrill was a true pioneer. For thirty-three years he flew as a commercial airline pilot, logging more than 36,000 flying hours and more than eight million air miles in his illustrious career.

Merrill attended the University of Mississippi where he played baseball and attracted attention as a rare pitcher able to throw both left- and right-handed, depending on the hitter he was facing. He reminded people of another ambidextrous pitcher of the time, Yale University's Dick Merrywell, and the similarity caused them to refer to Merrill as "Dick", a nickname that stayed with him for life. In 1914, flying overtook his enthusiasm for baseball and he tried to pursue it in France during World War I, but without success. After the war he learned to fly on a surplus Curtiss Jenny, a seventy-five mph training plane. He soon parted with his life savings to purchase a Jenny and it was the beginning of his life in aviation.

In 1928, Merrill became a pilot for what was then called Eastern Air Transport, destined to become Eastern Airlines. He was later referred to by Eastern boss Eddie Rickenbacker as "the best commercial pilot in the USA" and "the Captain's Captain." Merrill was one of the early leaders in the Air Line Pilots Association, helping to champion fair employment practices for airline pilots. He was also among the first commercial airline pilots to become proficient in the new system of instrument flying and he trained many other pilots in it.

Over time, Dick Merrill's other talents began to emerge—one being an exceptional and seemingly natural ability to relate to his passengers in a friendly and considerate way. He became a kind of good will ambassador—a role that Eastern was quick to exploit. In a time when few people had experienced flight and most were nervous at the prospect, Captain Merrill invariably displayed a sensitivity to their concerns. He admitted to vertigo when gazing down from a tall building, but was able to convince an anxious passenger that the motion of flying was much like sitting at home in a comfortable chair. He gave them the confidence they needed to become fliers and loyal customers of his airline.

With the advent of the Douglas DC-1 and DC-2, Dick Merrill determined to become rated and highly skilled in the operation of those and all subsequent aircraft to be used by Eastern. Both Merrill and Rickenbacker were persuaded of the need to replace the airline's obsolete equipment with the promising DC-2 transport to help bring Eastern out of a cycle of unprofitability. The two of them maintained close contact with Douglas engineers, influencing them in the design and development of both performance and passenger comfort of the new transport planes. Headroom, seat comfort, cabin soundproofing, lavatory and galley facilities, large windows, air circulation and heating, were all developed through the enthusiastic involvement of people like Rickenbacker and Merrill. Early in 1935, Eddie Rickenbacker ordered fourteen new DC-2s for Eastern to be operated mainly between New York and Miami and to be known as "The Great Silver Fleet."

In 1936 Merrill gained a measure of fame when, together with the entertainer and amateur pilot Harry Richman, he became the first commercial pilot to make a trans-Atlantic return trip. The pair flew a modified Vultee V-1 called *Lady Peace* and on the return flight were forced to land in Nova Scotia, short of their goal. Their adventure was later made into a Hollywood movie called *Atlantic Flight*, starring Merrill as himself.

Dick Merrill's concern for the safety and comfort of his passengers was always a priority and never more so than on a winter evening when he was bringing Flight Six into Newark on the final leg of a day-long trip that had begun in Miami at 8:30 that morning. The flight was due into the New Jersey airport at 5:05 p.m. and Merrill had plans to meet friends that evening at Toots Shor's in Manhattan.

Between Washington D.C. and Newark the weather deteriorated rapidly from "the possibility of a few snow flurries" to severe icing conditions. The engines of the DC-2 were running rough and vibration was increasing. Carburettor heat was "full open" and the control wheel vibrated and shook in Merrill's hands. The co-pilot aimed his flashlight beam at the right engine and propeller and yelled to his captain: "Holy Mackerel, we're sure icing up."

Radio communication with both ground stations and the company frequency were so broken by static in the storm that it was all but hopeless. Jack L. King describes the situation in his excellent biography of Merrill, *Wings of Man, The Legend of Captain Dick Merrill*: "Rather than take his passengers back to Washington, perhaps by descending to a lower altitude he might find a 'sucker hole' or establish ground contact. If there was enough ceiling and visibility he could find Newark by visual reference, since he was quite familiar with the New York area.

"The engine roughness seemed to increase as he began descending. Occasionally pushing the propeller speed to 'take-off rpm' helped sling ice from the propellers and smooth out the vibration. He was aware this sudden surge of power and noise would register a feeling of apprehension among his eight passengers. They had adjusted well to the relatively rough ride up the east coast, but after departing Washington the turbulence intensity had increased to moderate.

"Descending through 2,000 feet Merrill looked out his side

WHEN BILL LITTLEWOOD OF AMERICAN AIRLINES SUPERVISED THE BUILDING OF THE DOUGLAS SLEEPER TRANSPORT AT DOUGLAS AIRCRAFT IN THE 1930S, HE SAW TO THE ADOPTION OF A NEW FLIGHT INSTRUMENT, THE AUTOMATIC PILOT. PILOTS AND DOUGLAS ENGINEERS, FOR WHATEVER REASON, NICKNAMED THE GADGET "GEORGE" AND THE PILOTS CAME TO TRUST IT WITH THEIR LIVES AND THE SAFETY OF THEIR AIRCRAFT.

window hoping to see at least a dim glow through the clouds of New York City. Only a black void registered. He would make it back to Newark if he distinguished the lights of Broadway or any other lighted check point. He levelled at 1,500 feet and flipped on the left landing light again to observe flight conditions. The windshield appeared opaque from the heavy accumulation of wet snow. From the side window he could observe large blobs of snow mixed with sparkles reflecting from mixed rain racing toward the shaft of light. The reflected glow also confirmed a heavy accumulation of ice on the wing leading edge and prop dome. He noticed the accumulation was not smooth as usual, but had spurs of inverted icicles protruding in a porcupine configuration. He concluded they now had a mixture of rime and clear ice mixed with snow.

"The aircraft controls were responding sluggishly as Merrill pushed the throttle levers up to maximum continuous power. The manifold pressure gauges climbed erratically but the roughness persisted. Airspeed dropped slowly from 120 to 110 mph as he rolled in more 'nose up' elevator trim to maintain altitude. The co-pilot was still frantically attempting to identify any range station as he slowly cranked the full range on the LF receiver. He now had both ear pieces pulled down over his head. 'Any luck yet?' Merrill yelled.

" The flustered co-pilot knew what the captain was interested in, even though he only heard the muffled yell through his snug ear pieces. 'Can't get a damn thing but static,' was the reply. Merrill glanced back at the flight instruments and noted the rate of climb indicator was registering a sink rate of about 50 feet per minute. He rolled in more 'nose up' trim and the airspeed stabilized at 100 mph. The penalty of ice was developing into a serious problem. Not only was gross weight increasing but aerodynamic airflow had been altered.

"The control wheel was vibrating in his left hand as he gripped the throttle knobs with his right. He decided it was time to shed ice from the props again, and as he pushed the control knobs to 'high rpm', pelting slugs slung from the unbalanced blades impacted both sides of the cabin with the sound of a giant popcorn popper.

"Merrill continued to glance out his side window, hoping to discover a break in the clouds or pick up some kind of lights from the ground. During the past, he had been fortunate in this respect. Before any type of radio navigation was available, finding

a sucker hole as a way out of the clouds was standard operating procedure. He figured the key was ground contact. The odds were not favourable. Darkness, heavy snow, turbulence, precip, static, and now a heavy load of ice were cards from nature's stacked deck. He soon convinced himself the wisest action would be to reverse course and head south before the transport quit flying. First, just a few more minutes to look around for a hole in the clouds . . .

"Suddenly, there was a loud scraping noise as the aircraft brushed the tops of several trees. Merrill instinctively eased the control wheel back and pushed the throttle wide open. A microsecond later, impact noises exploded around the transport as tree limbs cracked about the cockpit area. Reacting to the imminent crash, Merrill chopped the power to 'idle' and immediately pulled the control column back into his stomach with both hands.

"The sound of crumpling metal and splintering trees echoed from the ridge as the 'Florida Flyer' severed a wide swath of small trees and saplings before settling to rest in a jungle of dense undergrowth. Flight Six had terminated on a mountain slope near Port Jervis, New York, some 50 miles north of its destination.

"The ship's wings had taken most of the impact and the cabin remained intact with very minor damage. The slow speed and nose high attitude necessary to carry the load of ice had provided an advantageous angle of impact, allowing the underside of the aircraft to absorb much of the blow. Unfortunately, as the aircraft decelerated gradually through the densely wooded area, a large broken tree limb had shattered the left windshield. A broken limb stub had hit Merrill a glancing blow to the mouth and dislodged several front teeth.

"An eerie silence settled momentarily over the huge metal capsule embedded among the snarled underbrush. The lights had shorted out soon after impact. The pilots grabbed their flashlights and stumbled toward the cabin area.

" 'Everybody okay?' one of the passengers yelled. Everyone answered in the affirmative. The co-pilot unlatched the outside cabin door to make sure it was not jammed. As it swung out, the swirling snow came through the opening and he grabbed the door and yanked to close it again. There were no fumes in the cabin from ruptured fuel tanks, but Merrill suggested the passengers refrain from smoking. One of the passengers, W.T.

Critchfield, decided it was time to praise the captain for his expert airmanship. Merrill attempted to change the subject and assure the passengers they would be taken care of. The conversation soon changed to the lighter side as several passengers admitted they were not fully aware the aircraft had actually crashed.

"It was not long before local residents located the crash site and reported the location to Eastern's anxious Newark Airport office. Carlton Bucher was on duty and recalls making a call to Captain Eddie Rickenbacker at his New York apartment. The dynamic airline president lost little time in getting a rescue party underway.

"When Rickenbacker arrived at the crash site, he wanted to hear a first-hand report from Merrill, but had trouble holding a conversation. Critchfield, the over-enthusiastic passenger, kept interrupting to praise Merrill's extremely fortunate landing as a masterpiece of flight technique! Rickenbacker informed Merrill the weather forecasts had been wrong. The southwest flow had provided a tailwind over twice the speed they had initially anticipated for the flight. Other passengers joined in as each praised Merrill's expertness at the controls, which they credited to saving their lives.

"Rickenbacker was amazed that the injuries were only minor. Other than Merrill's few missing teeth, the co-pilot and two passengers were the only ones to report slight bruises.

"After analyzing all the factors leading to the crash, Rickenbacker told the media there was a need to improve the DC-2's de-icing system, eliminate precipitation static, provide better weather and winds aloft forecasts and improve navigation aids if accidents of this nature were to be avoided in the future. Rickenbacker added that skill had indeed been a factor with his famed transatlantic pilot at the controls. He later remarked to the rescue team that 'Merrill was the luckiest damn pilot flying for Eastern.' This opinion would develop as an important factor in their future relationship.

"Merrill admits, over four decades later, that perhaps his pride for his record of not cancelling trips might have been a factor in causing him to be slightly 'over-confident.' He still emphasizes it was the ruggedness of the plane, rather than his skill, which accounted for all eleven people being alive after the crash. With blue eyes sparkling, he recalls with a grin, 'I was in Toots Shor's place by midnight.' "

KEEPING HER UP

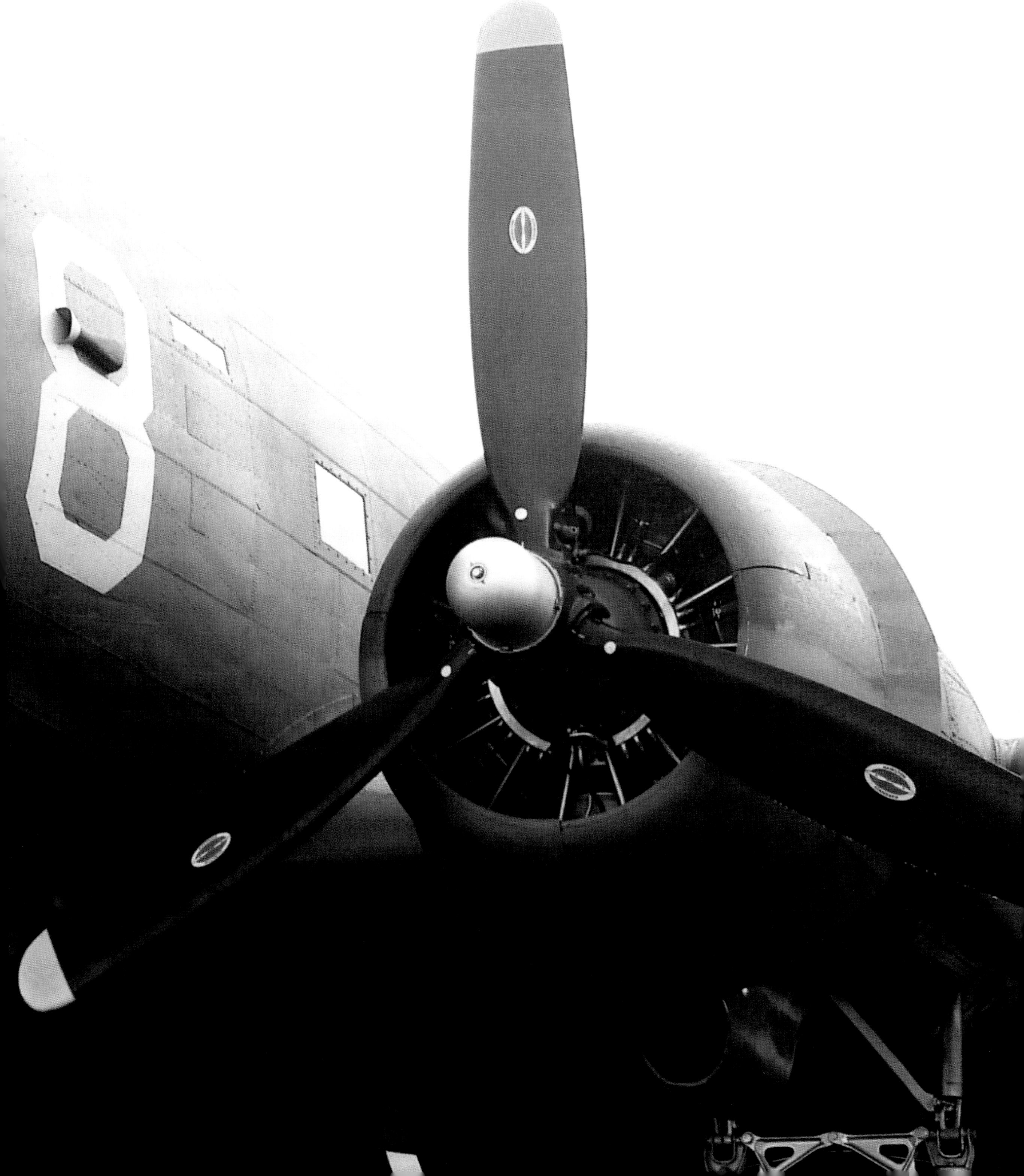

Franco Tambascia has worked for Personal Plane Services as an aeronautical engineer for eleven years. For much of that time he has helped care for the C-47 N1944A—an important aircraft in the collection of shipping executive Peter Livanos.

"The C-47 is a lovely aeroplane. Quite a lot of man-hours go into maintaining it. For every flight we have to oil-prime both of the engines, making sure there is oil all the way round each engine before we do the start. We get her out of the hangar, turn her over, start her up, warm the engines and then we're ready to go. In general, the maintenance on it is easy work, but it can be difficult in places.

"When we oil-prime, we use a kettle which heats the oil. Then we pump it through. We pull the props through 'fifteen blades' and then remove the sump drain and case drain, which allows oil to come out as well as go in. We can then monitor the oil coming out as well as going in, to make sure we've got clean oil going out and warm oil going in. We need to make sure we don't exceed 70 psi when we are hand-pumping, otherwise, we could blow the seals into the engine. We do this on every start-up. Normally, we then go flying. Once we've done the oil-prime, we have to run the engines within four hours; or, it being a radial, all the oil will drain back down to the sump and we want the oil at the top of the engine. In a start, the engines blow out loads of white smoke that cakes the whole under side of the aircraft in oil and this takes hours to clean up.

"Besides me, Tom Woodhouse is also a crew chief for the C-47. It's important to have a crew chief on board—an engineer available in case anything happens and the aeroplane gets stuck on another airfield. We always take an engineer and some tools and we do any necessary on-board maintenance as we go along.

"When our C-47 first came over to the UK, it didn't have the parachute-seat interior. We did all that restoration here at Personal Plane Services. In those days, the aircraft used to be kept at Wycombe Air Park and whenever we needed to do maintenance, we used to bring it round to the front of the hangar. If we were doing work on the engines, we'd open the hangar doors and put the aircraft facing into the hangar, with the engines inside and the wings outside. If we were doing any internal work on the fuselage, we'd turn the aircraft around and bring the tail-end inside.

"When the plane came here, the interior of the fuselage was all made of fibreglass matted sheet. The owner wanted it re-done in its D-Day configuration, which was a bit of a job. We took all of the interior out. It was all screwed to the airframe and behind it there was loads of insulation for soundproofing. We removed everything down to the old skins and then had to rub it all down, clean everything up, prime it and put it into the drab green colour. We located another DC-3 in the States, with all the parachute troop seats in it. We acquired the seats, brought them to the UK, restored them and fitted them into our aircraft—making it as it is today.

"We painted the aircraft here at PPS. We had all but the tail-end of it in the hangar, shut the doors against it and made a plywood cut-out of the fuselage cross-section so we could close the hangar up. We removed a window from the front of the fuselage, and put a ducting tube through it to draw out the paint fumes and then painted all of the interior of the plane. We then fitted the seats and the aircraft was moved to Kemble where it could be hangared for protection. For a while it resided at Hullavington and now it is based at Oxford.

"As for on-going maintenance, every year the aeroplane has to have an Event Four—a 100-hour total de-panel inspection. We drain the oil from both engines and do compression checks on them. There is a maintenance schedule that has been written for the aircraft and approved by the FAA; it's a checklist. We remove the exhausts, make sure there are no cracks in them, check all the fuel filters, hydraulic filters, carburettor filters, check for corrosion of the aircraft, check the flying controls, jack the aircraft up and do a retract test on the ground. Every five years the propellers have to be removed for overhaul. Even if the aircraft has only flown a few hours during the preceding year, the entire annual inspection has to be done. We do twenty-five-hour inspections as well. The annual is done in March each year. We take the aeroplane off-line to do the check, which takes about five weeks to complete. We have to de-panel the wings, check and tighten the wing bolts. There are about 350 odd bolts to check/tighten. It's quite a lot of work. For safety, we do things exactly as it says in the book and make sure that every nut and bolt is checked. And, whenever we have a snag or defect, it is noted in the tech log of the aircraft, which is maintained with every flight. Whenever such a defect is written up, we rectify it before the aeroplane flies again."

Andrew Davenport: "I hold a display authorization to fly the aircraft down to 100 feet. We don't attend the major airshows as a rule. The owner is happy for the aeroplane to go to events which aren't particularly well supported, and as the aeroplane doesn't have to earn a living, what money that we do make from appearing goes to military charities. My initial brief was to 'put a smile on people's faces', and we've done that for many people who flew C-47s and DC-3s in both the military and civilian world. They are so happy to see the aeroplane because it's such a rare sight these days. It's nice too, when we can get some of the World War Two veterans to come along. Obviously, they are getting fewer and fewer. If there is an event that is going to be attended by people who flew these aircraft or worked on them, it's great that we are able to show them the aeroplane on the ground and in the air. Apparently, it smells the same as it did in the 1940s. We, as crew, get a buzz out of seeing these people's faces—and the faces of youngsters who are used to getting on an Airbus or Boeing and cannot believe thAt people actually went on their holidays in these aeroplanes, let alone to war.

"The owner is very safety conscious. If there is anything that needs doing on the aeroplane relating to safety or to keeping it airworthy, he is quite happy to spend the money. We've probably got one of the best engineered DC-3s around. We're not operating commercially, but we maintain it to commercial standards. We maintain it to a higher degree than is required by the authorities.

"The owner's primary interest in the aircraft is its provenance and history. The fact that we know where it went, who it dropped, where it was in the formation—the sense of responsibility I feel because of its history—makes me very cautious about how we operate and what we decide to do.

"Next year is the sixty-fifth anniversary of D-Day and Arnhem, and we are hoping that we can take part in some parachute dropping over Normandy and Arnhem because that may be the last chance for some of the surviving veterans to travel over there. There is talk of maybe ten or more DC-3s/C-47s making mass drops over both locations. So, that's the next big milestone for us. I've got nothing but respect for the men who flew these aeroplanes in combat because they were dropping parachutists from maybe 400 or 500 feet, under fire. At least the troops in the back could get out of the aeroplane relatively quickly if necessary. There is no way I can see that both pilots could bale out if the aeroplane was severely damaged at low level. When we appear at shows and talk to people, I like to ensure that they understand that it was not only the paratroopers in these aeroplanes who were in mortal danger, but also the crews flying them. So, we will continue doing what we're doing. We don't want to thrash the aeroplane or crew every weekend. We'll pick the right sort of shows and events and maybe do ten a year or so. What we'll do in the interim is try and fly the aeroplane as regularly as we can, to keep it healthy and the crew current."

THE C-47A N1944A OVER HER D-DAY AIRFIELD, UPOTTERY, DEVON, IN THE SUMMER OF 2008.

257

THE WINGS VENTURE C-47A
N1944A ON THE FOLLOWING
FOUR PAGES, OVER OXFORD-
SHIRE IN JANUARY 2009.
WITH HER PILOTS ANDREW
DAVENPORT AND JOHN DODD
AT THE CONTROLS, THIS
HISTORIC AIRCRAFT APPEARS
AT AIRSHOWS AND OTHER
EVENTS FOR THE ENTER-
TAINMENT AND EDUCATION
OF ENTHUSIASTS AND THE
GENERAL PUBLIC WHO
THRILL TO THE SPLENDID
SIGHT AND SOUND OF HER.

"ON A DAY WHEN WE ARE GOING TO FLY THE AERO-PLANE, THE FIRST THING WE LOOK AT IS THE WEATHER. IT'S THE FIRST PRIORITY FOR ALL AVIATORS. WE'VE GOT VERY STRICT CRITERIA FOR HOW WE OPERATE. WE TRY TO PICK OUR ROUTE WHERE THE WEATHER IS GOING TO BE BEST, AND, IF WE ARE GOING TO LAND SOME-WHERE, WHERE THE WINDS FAVOUR THE RUNWAYS WE ARE GOING TO BE USING."
– ANDREW DAVENPORT

RIGHT: A DOUGLAS C-117D SUPER DC-3 AT HONOLULU INTERNATIONAL AIRPORT; LEFT: A U.S. NAVAL AIR TRANSPORT SERVICE R4D NEAR DUTCH HARBOR, ALASKA IN 1943. IN THE MONTHS FOLLOWING THE JAPANESE ATTACK ON THE AMERICAN NAVAL FACILITY AT PEARL HARBOR, HAWAII IN DECEMBER 1941, THREE NATS SQUADRONS WERE ESTABLISHED. BASED AT NORFOLK, VIRGINIA, OLATHE, KANSAS, AND OAKLAND, CALIFORNIA, THEIR INITIAL MISSION WAS TO RAPIDLY TRANSPORT VITAL CARGO, PERSONNEL, AND MAIL TO THE FLEET AND TO GROUND FORCES, PARTICULARLY IN ADVANCED AREAS OF OPERATION. BY THE END OF THE SECOND WORLD WAR, 26,000 PERSONNEL AND 540 AIRCRAFT WERE PROVIDING NATS SERVICES. NATS BECAME PART OF THE U.S. MILITARY AIR TRANSPORT SERVICE IN JUNE 1948.

RYAN FIELD IS SOUTHWEST OF TUCSON. THERE, IN THE DRY HEAT OF THE ARIZONA DESERT, RESTED THESE OLD C-47S IN THE 1960S.

ACKNOWLEDGMENTS

The author is grateful to the following people for their kind help in the development of this book and /or the use of their quoted material, photos, illustrations and other materials: Niklas Ahman, Stephen E. Ambrose, Geoff Barlow, Sigidur Benediktsson, Pia Bianchi, Tony Bianchi, Quentin Bland, Damien Burke, Rachel Connolly, Napier Crookenden, Lars Danielsson, Andrew Davenport, John Dodd, Dutch Dakota Association, Martin Evans, Stephen Fox, Oz Freire, Erik Frikke, Ernest K. Gann, Han Geurts, John Heggblom, Henry Holden, Eric Holloway, Hargita Kaplan, Neal Kaplan, John Keegan, Jack L. King, George R. Klare, Juha Klemettinen, Eric Koh, Michael Kominik, Geoff Lea, Peter Livanos, Fergus Mayhew, Margaret Mayhew, Eric Sevareid, Erik Sleutelberg, Doug Siegfried, C. Lachmund Sturm, Franco Tambascia, Simon Thomas, Ann and John Tusa, Paul Van Den Berg, Tom Woodhouse, Jerrold Wu. Special thanks to Simon & Schuster UK Ltd for the use of an excerpt from *Band of Brothers* © by Stephen E. Ambrose.

BIBLIOGRAPHY

Ambrose, Stephen E., *Band of Brothers*, Pocket Books, 2001.

Appleton, Victor, *Tom Swift and his Airline Express*, Grosset & Dunlap, Inc., 1926.

Bando, Mark, *101st Airborne*, Zenith Press, 2007.

Blair, Clay, *Ridgway's Paratroopers*, Naval Institute Press, 1985.

Borge, Jacques, and Viasnoff, Nicolas, *The Dakota*, Frederick Warne Ltd, 1980.

Bowers, Peter M., *The DC-3 50 Years of Legendary Flight*, Tab Books, 1986.

Brown, Austin J., *Douglas DC-3*, Ian Allan, 1993.

Burgett, Donald R., *Currahee!*, G.K.Hall & Co., 2000.

Burns, Dwayne T., and Burns, Leland, *Jump Into The Valley Of The Shadow*, Casemate, 2006.

Clancy, Tom, *Airborne*, Berkley Books, 1997.

Clarke, Bob, *10 Tons For Tempelhof: The Berlin Airlift*, Tempus, 2007.

Crookenden, Napier, *Airborne At War*, Ian Allan, 1978.

Devlin, Gerard M., *Silent Wings*, W.H. Allen, 1985.

Ethell, Jeffrey L., and Simonsen, Clarence, *The History of Aircraft Nose Art*, Motorbooks, 1991.

Glines, Carroll V., *The Amazing Gooney Bird*, Schiffer Publishing Ltd, 1996.

Gunther, John, *D-Day*, Harper & Brothers, 1944.

Holden, Henry, *The Douglas DC-3*, Tab Books, 1991.

Holden, Henry, *The Legacy of the DC-3*, Windcanyon Books, 2002.

Hooks, M. J., *Douglas DC-3 Dakota*, Winchmore Publishing Services Ltd, 1985.

Huschke, Wolfgang J., *The Candy Bombers*, Metrepol, 1999.

Ingells, Douglas J., *The Plane That Changed The World*, Aero Publishers, Inc, 1966.

Isby, David, *C-47/R4D Skytrain Units of the Pacific and CBI*, Osprey, 2007.

Jackson, Robert, *The Berlin Airlift*, Patrick Stephens, 1988.

Jones, Robert, *History of the 101st Airborne Division*, Turner Publishing, 2005.

London, Joanne Gernstein, *Fly Now!*, National Geographic, 2007.

Maguire, Jon A., *Gooney Birds & Ferry Tales*, Schiffer Publishing Ltd, 1998.

Marshall, S.L.A., *Night Drop*, Battery Press, 1962.

Miller, Roger G., *To Save A City: The Berlin Airlift 1948-1949*.

Morris, Eric, *Blockade: Berlin & The Cold War*, Hamish Hamilton, 1973.

Nordyke, Phil, *All American All The Way*, Zenith Press, 2005.

Nordyke, Phil, *The All Americans in World War II*, Zenith Press, 2006.

O'Leary, Michael, *DC-3 and C-47 Gooney Birds*, Motorbooks, 1992.

Parrish, Thomas, *Berlin in the Balance*, Perseus Books, 1998.

Pearcy, Arthur, *A Celebration of the DC3*, Airlife Publishing, 1985.

Pearcy, Arthur, *Berlin Airlift*, Airlife Publishing, 1997.

Pearcy, Arthur, *Dakota At War*, Ian Allan, 1982.

Pearcy, Arthur, *The Dakota*, Ian Allan, 1972.

Pearcy, Arthur, *Sixty Glorious Years*, Airlife Publishing, 1995.

Pearcy, Arthur, *Douglas Propliners DC-1 to DC-7*, Airlife, 1995.

Rathbone, A.D., IV, *He's In The Paratroops Now*, Robert M. McBride & Co., 1943.

Robson, Graham, *Propliner Renaissance*, Airlife Publishing, 2002.

Ruggero, Ed, *The First Men In*, HarperCollins Publishers, 2006.

Serling, Robert J., *When The Airlines Went to War*, Kensington Books, 1997.

Sevareid, Eric, *The Flying Humpty Dumpties*, Air News, Philip Andrews Pub. Co., and Reader's Digest, May 1944.

Shama, Rex H., *Pulse and Repulse*, Eakin Press, 1995.

Smith, Myron J., Jr., *Passenger Airliners of the United States 1926-1991*, Pictorial Histories, 1986.

Spencer, Otha C., *Flying The Hump*, Texas A & M University Press, 1992.

Szurovy, Geza, *Classic American Airlines*, Zenith Press, 2000.

Thorne, Bliss K., *The Hump*, J.B. Lippincott Co., 1965.

Tunner, William H., *Over The Hump*, Duell, Sloan and Pearce, 1964.

Tusa, Ann & John, *The Berlin Airlift*, Spellmount, 1988.

Urquhart, R.E., and Greatorex, Wilfred, *Arnhem*, Monarch Books, Inc, 1960.

Webster, David Kenyon, *Parachute Infantry*, Dell Publishing, 1994.

Young, Charles H., *Into The Valley*, PrintComm, Inc., 1995.

PICTURE CREDITS